Christopher Lloyd

GARDENER COOK

Christopher Lloyd
GARDENER COOK

Photographs by Howard Sooley

WILLOW CREEK PRESS

MINOCQUA, WISCONSIN

Gardener Cook
Copyright © Frances Lincoln Limited 1997
Text copyright © Christopher Lloyd 1997
Photographs copyright © Howard Sooley 1997

First Frances Lincoln edition: 1997

Published in the U.S.A. by WILLOW CREEK PRESS
P.O. Box 147, Minocqua, Wisconsin 54548 1–800–850–9453

ISBN 1 57223 136 X

Set in 12/15pt and 10/13pt Adobe Garamond Light
Typeset by Sandra Wilson
Printed in Hong Kong

PAGE 1 *Globe artichoke 'Gros Camus de Bretagne'*
FRONTISPIECE *Winter savory flowering on a wall-top at Great Dixter*

QUANTITIES
The recipes in this book are for six people, approximately (depending of course on appetite),
unless I have indicated otherwise.

CONTENTS

INTRODUCTION 6

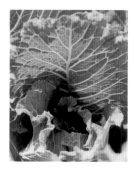

Introduction

*A*ny reader familiar with my writing might well wonder why cookery should enter into it. We have unlimited literature on cooking from professionals who know their subject from the inside. I firmly believe that, with very few exceptions, each of us is able to assimilate only one profession in a lifetime. That is because of the complexity of what we need to absorb.

I was into gardening right from the start, took to it professionally when I studied for a degree in Horticulture at Wye College, University of London; subsequently taught at the same college for four years as an assistant lecturer; returned home to Dixter; started a nursery and to make the garden a showpiece, and began writing articles and books on gardening.

Meantime, my mother and Mrs C., both of whom officiated in the kitchen, died in 1972 and 1975 respectively. My cooking repertory was very limited. When a child, I had prided myself on my chocolate buns, but they were always baked by a cook. I didn't understand that side of it, unsurprisingly, since we used a kitchener – a stove fuelled by coal – up to 1944, or thereabouts. Such stoves need understanding, in order to have the heat where and when you want it.

We then went over to electricity and have stayed with it. By the time I was left to cope, I was living alone in the house, but I loved to have friends to stay. My repertoire of fry-ups was far too limited and I found that to hire a cook for special occasions was expensive. The occasions were too numerous. Besides, I didn't really know what to ask for. So I started to study the subject, seeking the advice of friends and following written recipes. If you enjoy food, you want to be able to make good use of it.

We have always grown a lot of fruit and vegetables in the garden. What could be more natural than to want to use them effectively in the kitchen? As I gained confidence, the stream of friends visiting, largely at weekends, increased enormously and so did my enjoyment of them. I had the advantage of not having to cook for a family twice or more times a day, so there were, and still remain, periods when I could retrench and stop overeating (which is almost inevitable,

Pounding some chopped mint leaves in my kitchen

when you yourself produce tasty dishes). Even so, cookery was a hobby and always will be.

Still, after the sequence of growing things in the garden (in which I am staunchly supported by staff) and treating them in the kitchen (which I do wholly on my own) had been going on for twenty years, I did begin to feel that a book on these closely linked subjects might be a good idea.

Growing one's own food is tremendously rewarding, the product being, in most cases, so much tastier than anything on the market. When you start into cookery, you feel lost. Having all the items that make up a course, or indeed a meal, ready at the right moment, is bothering. One is grateful for recipes that allow food to be prepared in advance, so that it is possible to enjoy a pre-pran-dial drink with one's friends – surely the best moment in the day. But it is easy to go too far with reheating and keeping things hot. Straight from the stove or oven is often best. That's a small down-side in domestic cookery.

Incidentally, I never dish up. The food is served straight on to my guests' plates from the saucepans (or whatever) in which it was cooked. I hate those books that have glamorously laid out meals in violently coloured illustrations, which entirely put me off the product. I begged my publisher not to insist on that and when Howard Sooley was appointed photographer, I knew I was safe.

If the writer knows what he or she is writing about, not only from first-hand experience but from recent first-hand experience, it should not be difficult for the reader to follow any recipe. However, there are some authors of cookery books who are far more explicit (and reliable) than others, which is what the beginner needs. Later, we can move on to, possibly, more inspiring authors, who are apt to take some knowledge for granted. Jane Grigson quite often enjoins you to use soft butter. I knew of soft margarine and thought that soft butter must be a similar, marketable product. Well, of course, it merely means you need to have the butter in a warm enough condition to mix easily with other ingredients. So I was quite proud of myself once I was able to under-stand the language of recipes fairly easily.

I have not invented recipes of my own; merely adapted those that have been going around and that appeal to me. (There's nothing rare in that.) Often they don't even need adapting. Jane Grigson's writings are a great inspiration and I don't want to pretend that any of them are my own idea, so I have quoted her liberally and sometimes literally. As she herself wrote: 'In cooking originality is rare, it's all a matter of adjustment and balance.' She is a delight to read and nearly always expresses herself admirably. How sad that she died before we became intimate. She visited me at Dixter once. I gave her brill with a fishy sauce and was immensely proud that she declared me a good cook. That is a memory I treasure.

I have here only written of what I grow and what I have experienced. That means that many avenues remain unexplored, but at least it is an entirely personal book. Professional chefs reading it will doubtless snort at my stupidity on many occasions. I just hope that they will, on the whole, be charitable.

A book on such a subject should convey enjoyment. I have had so much from growing plants, from eating their products and from the social opportunities that cookery opens up, that I wanted to write about it and, perhaps, to strike an answering chord in some of my readers.

MY KITCHEN

My kitchen is unusual in some respects, by modern standards. It is very large; I get a lot of exercise simply by walking from one end to the other and back again (generally because my mind is insufficiently organized to save my feet). There is a long rectangular table in the centre and as great a working area as anyone could possibly wish for. How anyone manages in a tiny kitchen passes (my) belief.

Some of my friends are very helpful in the kitchen, peeling potatoes, trimming sprouts or whisking cream. I can talk to them so long as I am not following an exacting recipe. Company can be distracting. The only person with whom I can work concurrently on different recipes is my niece Olivia, and her company is a lot of fun. She tries out new recipes for me. Unfortunately, she lives abroad and I see all too little of her.

When I was a child, up to the age of twelve, when my father died, we had a cook, a kitchen maid, a lady's maid for my mother (usually French- or German-speaking) a parlour maid and a couple of house maids. They ate in the servants' hall, next to the kitchen, which is the obvious place to have a dining room, as it has been for me since our last resident servant left in 1944.

What with our family, the kitchen (and kitchen garden) had to cope with at least fourteen mouths, very often more. The coal-fuelled stove made it insufferably hot in summer, and the cook was generally subject to ill-temper. The kitchen swarmed with flies and wasps. Sticky fly-papers were hung from the ceiling. The wasps were trapped and drowned in special glass receptacles, baited with sweetened vinegar. Black-beetles (cockroaches) swarmed over the floor at night and there were traps for them. We children were awarded one penny for every black-beetle caught, but as they were trapped alive and had to be dealt with subsequently, this was not a popular task. I shall never let it be forgotten that it was DDT that got rid of our cockroach problem once and for all.

Nowadays, the kitchen is the coldest room in the house. Many of Jane Grigson's recipes assume that it will be warm and enjoin you to provide ice-cold water for making pastry dough, for instance. That is not a problem, at Dixter. The water runs ice-cold from the cold tap; also from the hot, for the first half-minute. Creaming butter and sugar together and making bread dough from fresh yeast present far greater problems. I resort to placing the mixing bowl or bread tins close to a wood fire at the other end of the house. Dahlia, my dachshund, ate the dough that was rising on one occasion. It continued to rise in her and she spent the most uncomfortable night in her life. But she would do it again.

There is a blow-heater in the kitchen – the dogs, Dahlia and Canna, seek comfort by lying in their bed in front of it and go into a semi-coma – but it doesn't really warm the kitchen when the weather is cold. Most families eat in their kitchens, but ours has two doors into the house at one end, at least one of them seldom closed (the world is divided between those who shut doors and those who leave them open); while at the other, an outside door leads into the kitchen yard, to the washing lines and to the building containing the deep freeze. Much as I like my kitchen, it is hard to think of it as a room.

The Aga-bores among my friends keep on at me about installing one, but when I am on my own, which I frequently am, how ridiculous that sort of non-stop heater would be. Besides, I should miss the old kitchener, even though I don't use it. The makers of my cooker no longer make them and I am told that I shall have to change it, but to what has not been decided. It is worth noting here that well-insulated modern cookers do not need to be set at temperatures as high as those given in recipes (for instance Jane Grigson's) written ten or twenty years ago. You will soon automatically adjust for the performance of your own oven.

My refrigerator is small, when the house is full, but it was made to last and dates from the early 1940s! Large refrigerators are always full, in my observation. Nature abhors a vacuum and food gets left in them when there should be a more regular turnover. With a small refrigerator, there is far less scope for this to happen.

It will be seen that in some matters I am old-fashioned. I don't even have a pressure cooker or a microwave, but I dote on the Magimix that Beth Chatto gave me, so mechanization is not unknown, at Dixter.

I am blessed with a wonderful housekeeper, Anne Jordan, who lays the table for me, washes up and sees to accommodation for the invading hordes (sometimes she is a little inclined to put a young man and woman into the same bed regardless of whether they are intimates). She never complains about there being too many of us; on the contrary, she always cooperates and the bigger the invasion, the happier she is.

I conclude this on a Sunday evening – the last day in March, when there have been nine of us to cook for over the weekend. Just before we open to the public, Fergus Garrett, my head gardener and closest friend, organizes a band of volunteers to help us get the garden ship-shape. I am confined to the kitchen, but no complaints on that score.

By Sunday afternoon, my duties are over and I can venture into the garden to do a little work there myself. Meantime, from the garden's produce, I have made artichoke and carrot soup. Leeks have accompanied boiled ham, together with fava beans, frozen when really young, in mid-July last year. A huge salad was largely composed of home-grown ingredients. 'Pink Fir Apple' potatoes accompanied Delia Smith's excellent fish pie. All in all, not a bad link between garden and kitchen, gardener and cook.

Fergus, who has enabled the gardens at Dixter to make huge forward strides, in the past few years

TWO BASIC RECIPES

Piecrust dough and stock are two items that crop up throughout my recipes and so I should like to say something about making them here. I also use various recipes for sweet pastry dough, either from Jane Grigson or given me by different friends. The ingredients and method for these I include in the recipes as they occur.

PIECRUST DOUGH

The method is always the same, even if the ingredients vary slightly. I generally make piecrust dough using a half-and-half mixture of lard and margarine (lard makes the piecrust shorter), unless I have a vegetarian guest, when I use all margarine.

¾ cup plus one tablespoon
all-purpose flour
2 tablespoons *each* margarine and lard *or*
4 tablespoons margarine
Pinch of salt
Cold water to mix

Sieve the flour and salt into a mixing bowl. Add the margarine and lard in small lumps. As margarine is harder than lard, it will need to come out of the refrigerator an hour or so earlier, to soften up.

Mix the fats into the flour with the tips of your fingers and thumbs. 'Reduce to fine crumb' is the accepted jargon, but I should warn that the crumb is not all that fine and if you continue too long, the process goes into reverse and the lumps become larger. The whole process takes little longer than a minute and should be done with a far-away look in your eyes while you contemplate eternity. A great moment. I love it.

Wash your hands, using a nail brush. To your crumb, add cold water – about 3 tablespoons. If too little, the dough will crack at the edges as you roll it out but will make the lightest pastry. With a metal spatula, start bringing the mixture together, cutting and turning. Finish with your hands (another ritual moment), which will not need flouring if they are cool, until you have a ball of dough that leaves the sides of the bowl cleanly.

At this point, most recipes instruct you to put the ball of dough in a plastic bag and leave it in the refrigerator or a cool place to rest. Instead, if conditions are cool, after gathering the dough into a ball, I roll it out, line the pie plate and then allow it to rest in our very cool larder. I find that the condition of the dough is, usually, more malleable and less likely to crack at the margins (like a Norwegian fjord) when being rolled out if this is done immediately. Otherwise it can easily become too hard and stiff. Neither do I normally find it necessary (using this method) to weight the dough to prevent it from bubbling when pre-baking.

When a recipe specifies 1½ quantities piecrust dough, make it with 1¼ cups all-purpose flour and a total of 6 tablespoons fat; for double quantity, use 1¾ cups flour and 8 tablespoons fat.

STOCK FOR SOUPS

I use the carcasses of most fowls, including game birds, for stock but where you don't want to mask the main flavour of a soup unduly, chicken, guinea fowl and turkey carcasses make the best choice.

Into a roomy cooking pot, put:

1 mature carrot, cut into chunks
1 medium onion, quartered
1 leek top (if in season)
1 thick slice of celeriac root, celeriac or celery leaf stalks, or failing these, part of a lovage leaf, to give the celery flavour
Parsley stalks
A sprig of thyme and winter savory
Other herbs, according to availability:
sorrel stalk, sprig of tarragon,
dill leaf, sprig of chervil

6 peppercorns
1 teaspoon salt

Weight all these down with the chicken/turkey/pheasant/guinea fowl/goose/duck carcass(es), broken up, and including any skin. (One of my friends collects and includes the bones from her diners' plates. I am a little squeamish about that.)

Cover with cold water, bring just to a boil and simmer with the lid not quite on for two hours. Strain. When cold, skim off the fat, place in sealed containers and freeze if not immediately required.

This makes quite concentrated stock; when light stock is called for I dilute it by half.

FRUIT TREES

Apricot

Peach

Mulberry

Plum

Fig

Pear

Apple

Quince

Medlar

Apricot

The flavour of home-grown apricots, even if they are not fully ripe, is unbelievably better than any you can buy in England. But, in our cool climate, it is a dead loss as a tree, unless we give it the added warmth of a sunny wall. Tie in as much growth as there is room for without branches overlapping and remove the very strong shoots that jut forward and are impossible to tie back.

If a large branch system becomes very old and tired, it may need removing and gradually replacing with new growth. Or a branch may, disconcertingly, die, but that does not affect the overall performance of the tree.

Our apricot must have been planted before the First World War (certainly before I was born) and it is still going strong. I have no idea which variety it

is, but the stock, which suckers but not too seriously, appears to be 'Brompton', which is vigorous. It is the first fruit tree to flower, in March; pure white blossom but with a reddish calyx. Although it always flowers well, cropping is spasmodic: sometimes bountiful, sometimes light, sometimes none. I always look anxiously for bees at work on it, but rarely see more than two or three, even though there are plenty of bees about. As the shadow of a bee against the wall is very like the bee itself, my count is apt to be over-optimistic.

PAGE 14 *Our apricot flowers in March*
PAGE 15 *Young 'Brunswick' figs developing in spring*

LEFT *A honey bee at work on the apricot blossom*
RIGHT *Apricots ripening on the sunny house wall*

In 1993, after Fergus Garrett had joined me as head gardener and everything began to seem possible instead of merely a pipe dream, we took a child's paintbrush and hand-pollinated the blossom. The subsequent crop was fantastic and had to be thinned. If you leave the fruits jostling one against another, not only will they be very small but if one goes bad the rot rapidly spreads to all the neighbours.

In California apricots are ripe in June; our fruit ripens in late July and early August. Where summers are cool, apricots grow well under barely heated or cold glass, trained against a wall or on wire, like peaches (see page 25).

The skin of an apricot is very soft and I do not find it necessary to skin them for any purpose. Juice runs freely, when you bite into a fruit. It is free-stoning and easily halved, even if not quite ripe. For jam and many recipes, the stones' kernels are used.

STEWED APRICOTS

Stewed apricots are excellent for breakfast. I cook them slowly at 140°C/275°F/gas mark 1 in a casserole in the oven, adding sugar to taste but no water. This way the fruit keeps its shape. Cooking takes about an hour. Most of this stewed fruit goes into the deep-freeze for reference through the year.

APRICOT JAM

Apricot jam has many uses besides the obvious one of eating it with bread (see opposite for *Apricot Glaze*). When making it, I use the unriper fruits from a picking and, as the jam does not set that easily, I add a little tartaric acid to the fruit when boiling it down. The amount of sugar is rather less than is generally recommended, but I consider most jams and marmalades to be over-sweet. Makes about 7lb jam.

5lb apricots (stoned weight)
2 teaspoons tartaric acid (optional)
3lb sugar
Water

Put the apricots, with the tartaric acid if you are using it to assist setting, into a preserving pan. Don't make the mistake of adding a lot of water: the fruits will soon make a great deal of fluid of their own, and any extra water simply has to be evaporated before the sugar is added, otherwise the jam won't set. So don't quite cover the fruit. Add as many of the apricot kernels as you have the time and patience to extract (place each pit on a brick or stone and cover with a cloth before you bash it with a hammer). Bring to a boil and cook until the pulp is thickish, about an hour. Stir in the sugar, preheated in a low oven. Once it has dissolved, raise the heat and boil

18

hard, stirring at frequent intervals to pre-vent it sticking.

Meantime, put a plate in the refrigerator to get cold. After 20 minutes, dip a wooden spoon into the jam, lift it to the horizontal and watch whether the liquid drops off the edge without hesitation, or whether it has a tendency to flake before each drop falls. If the latter, drip a little on to your cold plate and return it to the refrigerator. After a minute, take the plate out and hold it against a light so that the light reflects off the sample's surface. Dip your finger lightly on to the surface and move it sideways. If the sample wrinkles along the surface in front of your movement, all is well; the jam

is ready. If not, return the pan to the heat for another minute or two and repeat the procedure.

Off the heat, allow the jam to rest for 15 minutes. This stops the fruit rising to the top of the jars, leaving only jelly at the bot-tom. Meanwhile, heat the clean, dry jars in a cool oven for 5 minutes. While they are hot, fill them with the jam to within ½in of their rims. Wipe each rim with a clean, damp cloth to remove any spills, then seal. Most recipes advocate covering with waxed discs and cellulose jam pot covers, but I just screw the lid tightly on the jar. Store in a cool, dark place.

A P R I C O T   G L A Z E

An apricot glaze brushed over a fruit tart (see page 27) gives it a good, glistening finish. Turn out some of your apricot jam into a heavy pan and add a little water. Stir

over medium heat until dissolved. Pass through a fine sieve and add a little lemon juice to taste. Brush the warm glaze over the cold tart.

S T E A M E D   P U D D I N G   W I T H   A P R I C O T   J A M

Unfashionable though they may be, I love steamed puddings and so do all the friends, including the French, who meet them here. For lightness, I use bread-crumbs rather than flour. It is unnecessary to add baking powder or baking soda. This quantity serves 4.

1 stick butter, softened
Generous ½ cup sugar
2 eggs
Finely grated zest of 1 orange
4 tablespoons apricot jam
1 teaspoon ground cinnamon
2 cups fresh breadcrumbs

Butter a 5-cup, deep, heatproof bowl. Cream the butter and sugar with a wooden spoon or an electric beater. Beat in the eggs. Add the orange zest, apricot jam and cinnamon. Fold in the breadcrumbs. Turn into the bowl. Tear off a sheet of foil, dou-ble it over and make a central pleat to allow for the expansion of the pudding. Tie on the foil with string, looped into a knot at one end and pulled tight with a slip knot threaded through the loop. (I use the same string over and over.) Steam for 2 hours. I always use a double boiler. Alter-natively, place the bowl in a pan of boiling water with the water reaching half-way up

Apricots almost ready to eat

the sides. Check the water level from time to time and top it up if necessary.

After 2 hours' steaming, remove the bowl from the boiler, pull the free end of your knot and remove the foil. Loosen the pudding from the sides of the bowl with a metal spatula. Place a warmed, broad-based plate over the top of the pudding and (protecting your hands) invert the whole thing deftly, with a rolling motion towards you.

APRICOT AND ALMOND CRUMBLE

Jane Grigson gives this recipe both in the *Fruit Book* and in *English Food*, and it is excellent served hot or cold. I make the crumble using slightly less sugar and butter than she gives in her recipe.

Fresh ripe apricots
¼ to scant ½ cup sugar
½ cup blanched, split almonds

Crumble
1 cup all-purpose flour
Scant ½ cup sugar
1 cup finely ground blanched almonds
1 stick butter, well chilled and diced

Halve the apricots, having taken enough to cover the bottom of a shallow baking dish (which depends on their size). Extract the kernels from the pits, chop them coarsely and scatter over the fruit, along with the sugar. To make the crumble, mix the flour, sugar and ground almonds. Cut in the butter and spread over the fruit evenly.

Arrange the split almonds on top (I often forget them and it doesn't much matter). Bake in a preheated oven at 180°C/350°F/ gas mark 4 for about 40 minutes, till the top is browned.

OLD-FASHIONED APRICOT TART

Adapted from *Jane Grigson's Fruit Book.* You can use either rich piecrust dough or the sweet pastry dough she calls creamed *pâte sucrée*. Serves 6 to 8.

Enough apricots to cover the pastry in a
single layer (this will be more than you
had expected, maybe 30 or 40)
Light syrup made from 1½ cups sugar and
2½ cups water
1¼ cups cream, either whipping, adding
lemon juice to sharpen it, or one-third
sour cream and two-thirds heavy
2 extra-large eggs
Sugar
4 tablespoons butter
Confectioners' sugar

Sweet pastry dough
1 stick butter, soft but cool
2 rounded tablespoons vanilla sugar
1 extra-large egg
Pinch of salt
2 cups all-purpose flour

To make the pastry dough, cream the butter and sugar. Beat in the egg and salt and, when the mixture is reasonably well amalgamated, add the flour. The dough should need no water. Put it in a plastic bag and rest in the refrigerator or a cool place for at least 30 minutes.

I find this dough extremely fragile to handle. A friend suggests the following

method. On a floured cloth, roll out the dough to fit an 8in tart pan. Turn the cloth upside down on to the pan. Press the dough into the sides and trim off the excess. Leave to rest again, for 30 minutes to an hour.

Place a baking sheet in the oven and preheat to 180°C/350°F/gas mark 4. Pre-bake the tart shell for 10 to 15 minutes, until it is just firm but not brown.

Meanwhile, halve the apricots, discarding the pits. Poach the fruits lightly in the simmering syrup until tender but still in good shape (2 minutes at most, if they were ripe). Remove with a draining spoon, allow to cool and arrange, cut side uppermost, on the pastry in concentric circles.

Beat the cream(s) with the eggs, sweetening to taste. Melt the butter and pour it in warm. Pour this mixture gently on to the fruit (you may not need it all; it depends on the depth of the crust). Bake for 40 minutes or so, until the filling is just set firm.

Boil down the apricot cooking liquid to make a very thick, syrupy glaze. When the tart comes out of the oven, let it cool a minute or two. Dab the glaze all over with a brush, without disturbing the fruit, 'to make it look shiny and even more delightful'. Dust the pastry rim (if there is one) with confectioners' sugar.

Peach

A ripe peach from one's own garden is a special treat. You know that eating it will be a sticky, slobbery affair, so you lean forwards, allowing the inevitable drips to fall on the ground rather than on your clothes. Then you lick your fingers and wipe them as best you may. But they won't resume normality until washed.

The peaches we grow in England are white and extremely free with their juice. If ripe, they peel easily, like the cap of a mushroom. If not entirely ripe, they peel on the rosy, sunny side only. In this condition, they can be peeled readily by pouring boiling water on them in a bowl, draining them after half a minute, then peeling. The imported peaches that I buy are usually yellow-fleshed; they hold their juice and are readily skinned, even when ripe, only after the boiling water treatment.

Nectarines are a smooth-skinned type of peach, having the advantage that you can eat the skin without noticing. But they tend to be small, hard and fibrous when grown outside in Britain. My father grew 'Lord Napier'; it was never a success. The protection of a cold greenhouse makes all the difference, producing ambrosial fruit.

I have never grown peaches or nectarines under glass myself, but my eyes bear witness to the depredations of red spider mites under these circumstances, causing the foliage to become pale and papery, eventually falling prematurely. Dry heat promotes this pest. The trees will need daily syringing with cold water, in warm weather often more than once. Attention must also be paid to generous watering at the root, especially if the roots cannot reach outside the base of the greenhouse and into the garden.

Although peach trees are hardy, their wood needs hot summer weather if it is to ripen. Unripened growth is inclined to die back. So, where the summer is cool, peaches are normally grown against a warm wall with an aspect between southwest and southeast. However, even in England, if we are lucky with our season, they can ripen good crops as small, free-standing trees. The lack of a suitable wall is not necessarily cause for despair, particularly in a sheltered town garden.

Rosy and ripe on the sunny side, this peach is still green where it has been shaded by a leaf

A wall-trained peach in flower

My grandmother had two such trees in her Putney garden, London SW15, and they fruited well. Furthermore, she had raised them herself from peach pits. This method of propagating peaches is not normally recommended, as the result is uncertain, but it is sometimes irresistible. The sensible gardener will buy a grafted sample of a true-to-name and recognized variety. 'Peregrine' is the best known, but there are plenty of others available, early (July), mid-season and late (into October).

Flavour depends almost entirely on the season and on the amount of sun that each fruit has received. The redder its skin, the sweeter and more aromatic its flesh will be. Even one leaf laid across the fruit while ripening will leave a pale mark on the skin beneath it.

The ripening date will also vary, within the same variety by as much as a month. My father, who visited St Andrews for golf every August and early September, had the peaches and early pears at Dixter boxed up in wooden crates and sent to him by rail. That was between the wars. In recent hot summers our peaches have mostly ripened in July.

Peaches do get seriously damaged by birds, wasps and, in a droughty season when water is in short supply, by honey bees, which swarm over a damaged surface in search of sweet moisture. They will attack late raspberries in like manner. In the old days, my mother made protective bags out of mosquito netting (mosquito nets were a feature of my childhood), but peaches lie so closely against the supporting branch that fixing bags efficiently is a problem. I don't bother. The result is that a lot of damaged peaches enter the kitchen. Having removed the damaged parts, their skins and stones, I stew them with sugar and freeze them. Peaches, apricots and plums make a change from my usual breakfast of stewed 'Bramley's Seedling' apples.

WALL PEACHES

A great deal has been written about the cultivation, especially the pruning and training, of wall peaches. I'm after a crop, not a work of art, which a properly fan-trained peach admittedly is, with every branch evenly spaced from its neighbour, the same method being used for peaches grown under glass. The best support against the wall is with permanent wires stretched in parallel, either horizontally or vertically, between vine eyes. For ties you need only use a thin, unprotected, two-ply fillis twine, which will have strength and durability enough to last one season – the annual pruning entails the removal of 90 per cent of the previous year's ties, so there's no point in using anything more substantial.

Plant in autumn (for preference) or winter, in well-drained, well-prepared ground that has been allowed to settle. The tree should be set about 4in in front of the wall, the graft union being well clear of the ground. Plant, in fact, at the same level as the 'tide mark', which shows the level at which the plant grew in the nursery.

Fruiting should not be expected for the first couple of years. During that time, train in the young growths at an even spacing. Never allow branches to cross, as the top one will shade out the stem beneath it, when both are in leaf. All through its life, a certain number of strong, sappy water shoots will be made from the centre of the tree, that cannot be readily tied in, partly because they face forwards and partly because there is seldom the space for them. It is helpful if, when very young and soft in late spring or early summer, they are pinched back to four leaves, this operation being repeated during the summer, whenever more such growth is initiated. What remains will eventually be removed at the winter pruning, but that will have been made a much simpler and less drastic affair.

Most of a peach's flowers and fruit are borne on young, unbranched stems grown in the previous summer. There are also short spur growths which will bear fruit, but the first described are what should be encouraged and I remove most spurs when pruning in winter (late winter – it's nice to feel the sun on your back). When these stems have fruited (ideally, each should be allowed no more than two fruits, but that will entail early summer thinning), they will be removed, unless the subsequent extension growth from their tips is need-ed, in the early years, to increase the tree's framework. When removing these fruited stems, take each back to the young shoot which will be located near the base. That shoot will be tied in to provide the next crop of fruit. Normally it will be some 15in to 18in long and you'll be able to identify the incipient flower buds along it.

When tying in, you will aim at an even coverage and spacing against the wall. It is best to work from the outside inwards, from the right to the centre and likewise from the left. Each stem may need two ties. Visualize it weighted with fruit and make sure that the top tie is sufficiently close to the end of the shoot for any developing fruit to be behind it. If in front, the fruit will be waving about, largely unsupported.

The only other attention that my trees receive is spraying against the fungus (*Taphrina deformans*) causing the hideous disease leaf curl. This appears, with its unmistakable red pustules, on the young foliage in mid-spring. Affected leaves are shed; sometimes every leaf on the tree. A fresh crop will ensue, but it may be imagined how weakening this murrain is. I must add, however, that a garden owner I met in Victoria, British Columbia, had a large and productive peach in his garden, which he never sprayed, regularly losing its foliage, yet it cropped well.

But I do recommend preventive measures, though they don't always work. Spray with a fungicide in autumn, around leaf fall, and again in spring (twice, for preference, if the weather has been wet), before the tree's flowering. We sometimes spray again after it, too. At the same time you can include any almonds in your garden. They, too, are susceptible. Blossom wilt disease is also rife, in wet weather, on Morello cherries and various ornamental cherries such as *Prunus tomentosa* and *P. glandulosa* 'Alba Plena'. They can be protected with the same spray and at the same time. It is wet weather which decides whether leaf curl will be a menace. If, with overhead protection at this critical winter and early spring season, you can provide the tree with shelter, so that its branch system remains dry, there will be no problem. Peaches grown under glass are not susceptible to leaf curl.

Peaches are self-pollinating, but in bad weather and under glass they can do with helping, going from flower to flower with an artist's paintbrush. I don't. Neither do I protect against frost during the tree's flowering. I should, of course. If netting is draped across the tree, it must be coarse enough to allow bees to reach the blossom.

When deciding whether a peach is ripe, for heaven's sake don't press your thumb into its flank, thereby leaving a nasty bruise. Press very gently, close to the stalk, if you must. If you grasp the whole fruit (gently) in your hand and (gently) pull, a ripe fruit will detach without being damaged. The ripening of a tree's fruit will often extend over several weeks. The difference in flavour between a fruit culled at exactly the right moment from your own tree and one picked weeks before ripe for the sake of marketing, has to be experienced to be believed.

The following recipes come from *Jane Grigson's Fruit Book* and have been applied with my own peaches, picked in the second half of August.

BROILED PEACHES

Cut the peaches in half and remove the pits. Brush the cut sides with melted butter and sprinkle generously with sugar. Broil cut side up, gently at first to heat the peaches through, then more fiercely to brown the sugar. Serve hot with vanilla ice-cream, or with whipped cream.

PEACH TART

Use plain piecrust dough so that you can cook the tart at a high heat without the pastry burning.

1½ quantities piecrust dough (see page 12)
peaches

Roll out the piecrust dough and use it to line a 10in tart pan. Scatter the dough trimmings chopped into coarse, even crumbs over the bottom. Leave to rest in the refrigerator or a cool place for 30 minutes.

Put a baking sheet in the oven and pre-heat to 220°C/425°F/gas mark 7. Quarter the fruit or cut it into eighths, retaining the skins. (If using your own fruit, it may be easier to slip the skins off.) Set the pieces, skin side down, tightly together in concentric circles on the pie shell. Add no sugar. Place the tart pan on the hot baking sheet. (The quick surge of heat will help ensure a crisp base.) Bake for about 25 minutes, until the tips of the fruit are lightly caught with brown. Check from time to time. If the pastry looks like burning, protect with foil.

While the tart is still warm, brush it with thick sugar syrup or leave it to cool then brush with apricot glaze (see page 19).

PEACH FOOL

Peel 1lb peaches, blanching first in boiling water, if necessary. Chop them roughly. Melt 4 tablespoons butter in a saucepan, add the peach pieces and cook gently until they are soft enough to mash with the back of a large wooden fork. Add sugar to taste (you won't need much). Whip 1¼ cups heavy cream till floppy stiff. Fold in the fruit. Chill before serving (our larder is quite chilly enough, as a rule).

Mulberry

I have a special affection for mulberries, having been brought up and lived close to them all my life. My parents planted a well-matched pair of standards, on the made-up ground of a terrace, when the garden was created. It is of the black mulberry, *Morus nigra*, that I write, the only species worth growing unless you are a collector. Being in good soil, they grew fast and became too large for their positions. However, nature lent a hand and one of them, when particularly heavily laden with fruit one September, was irremediably torn asunder by an equinoctial gale. I did not replace it, but had a triangle of wire cables fixed to the upper crown of the remaining tree.

Came the storm of October 1987, when most of the tree disintegrated – but the cables may have prevented it from splitting down the centre of the trunk. This and part of one main branch survived and fantastic growth was made in the following year: up to 4ft of new wood. It is interesting that the leaves on young plants, especially seedlings, are heavily lobed. As the tree matures, the leaves adopt their normal adult heart shape. After the storm, the young growth reverted to the juvenile foliage shape, for a while.

The mulberry makes a beautifully shaped tree, perhaps an even greater pleasure to look at in winter than when heavy with summer foliage. It is adept at looking ancient, when, perhaps, no more than eighty years old (in this it resembles the common wisteria, *Wisteria sinensis*), and great antiquity has been ascribed to trees that deserve no more than a century to their credit. If heavy lateral limbs have been allowed to develop, they should be supported on wooden crutches, which can themselves be a picturesque feature. A mulberry's branches will come down to the ground, if unpruned. For the sake of mowing, some pruning is generally desirable.

Much disappointment is frequently caused when gardeners requiring a mulberry have failed to specify which kind. They may then be sold the white mulberry, *M. alba*, which has insipid fruit and is a tree lacking in character (though it is the best species for the raising of silkworms). Go to a reputable source to obtain your tree and ask for *M. nigra* 'Chelsea'. This will have been vegetatively propagated, probably from cuttings, and will start bearing fruit at an early age.

A seedling of this species is to be avoided, since its performance will be unpredictable. *M. nigra* bears male and female flower trusses, sometimes on

Our mulberry, Morus nigra, *in early spring*

separate branches (as can be seen on the specimen at Glyndebourne Opera, if you visit early in the Festival season), sometimes on separate trees. Should you obtain an all-male tree, it will never fruit. An all-female tree, however, is just what you need. If it has no pollinator, the fruit will have few or no pips. That's fine, and saves picking them out of your teeth.

Whereas black mulberries make handsome trees in the south of England, their wood fails to ripen further north, and they'll need to be trained against a warm wall. Even so, a specimen I know in Fife, grown this way, never fruits. However, in colder climates mulberries can be grown and fruited in large pots in a greenhouse.

PAGES 30–31 *The mulberry in young leaf*

The only disease which is likely to afflict a mulberry tree is a kind of canker, caused by a fungus. It generally attacks fairly young wood, 6in to 9in behind the tip of a shoot. When this is encircled, the shoot dies, the leaves turn yellow, then shrivel. The trouble is worst following a wet spring but generally corrects itself if the following year is normal.

Mulberries have the messiest fruit imaginable. The tree is best sited in grass; if overhanging a paved area, the fruit stains will remain till the end of the year. And don't visualize yourself sitting in the shade of your own mulberry much later than midsummer. There won't be any shade till the very end of spring, as mulberries flush late. Their leaves fall in mid-autumn, first becoming yellow. A night frost will result in all the leaves falling early the next morning, in a matter of an hour. This is an amusing drama, making a carpet so thick beneath the tree that no grass remains visible.

Pip Morrison, after gathering mulberries for a steamed pudding

EATING MULBERRIES

Although my mulberries begin to redden in July, they do not reach agreeable ripeness for eating raw much before the end of August. The fruit should then be dark red, verging on black, both sharp and sweet, causing a tingling sensation on the palate. There is plenty of competition from birds (starlings, blackbirds) and insects, but usually plenty left for us.

The mulberry is an aggregate of tiny fruits, clustered around a green stalk (which has to be spat out). To gather, the stalk must be detached from its supporting branch. Sometimes it comes away easily. As often, it does not. You exercise a little constraint, and the mess begins. However, members of our visiting public who have a taste for mulberries will spend half an hour at a time regaling themselves. Good luck to them.

In her *Fruit Book* Jane Grigson quotes a sauce, from Elizabeth David, to whom it was suggested by a sixteenth-century Italian recipe; she also mentions

A mulberry developing from flower to fruit

32

mulberry ice-cream. I have not succeeded with the ice-cream using raw mulberries (so successful with blackcurrants, see page 93), as what passes through the strainer is entirely liquid and includes no pulp. Probably a sorbet would be more successful, but I am not that keen on sorbets. Here is the sauce:

MULBERRY AND ALMOND SAUCE

An excellent sauce served (only just warm) with boiled, smoked ham on the bone. Doubtless it would go well with other meats, like boiled ox tongue.

¾–1lb mulberries
Generous ¾ cup sugar
¾–1 cup soft white breadcrumbs

About ½ cup finely ground blanched almonds

Cook the mulberries with the sugar, not too fast, until the juice flows. Mix the crumbs and almonds in a bowl, then add the mulberries, folding them in gently.

STEAMED MULBERRY SUET PUDDING

Steamed puddings go down very well in this house. With suet crust, the steaming time is longer than with an integrated pudding using breadcrumbs. This recipe for a steamed mulberry pudding is another from *Jane Grigson's Fruit Book*.

1lb mulberries
Sugar

Suet crust
4 cups self-rising flour
8oz grated suet
Pinch of salt
Cold water to mix

Butter a 5-cup, deep, heatproof bowl.

In a large mixing bowl, mix the flour and suet with your hands and add a pinch of salt. Add water, enough to make a soft, pliable but not sticky dough. If too much water has been added, correct with more flour. Gather into a ball which leaves the sides of the bowl cleanly.

Transfer to a pastry board and roll out into a circle. Remove a one-quarter sector of this circle and set aside for the lid. With the remainder, line your buttered bowl. Fill the cavity with mulberries, interspersing them with sugar. Judge the amount of sugar according to the ripeness of the fruit (approximately ½ cup sugar to each 1lb fruit).

Gather the dough set aside into a ball and roll it out for the lid. Using a pastry brush, moisten the two dough surfaces that will come together and apply the lid. Press the edges together. Now follow the instructions for covering and steaming given in *Steamed Pudding with Apricot Jam*, pages 19–20. Suet pudding needs steaming for at least 3 hours. In fact, I steam for 6 hours, if I have the time, as this enables the suet crust to become crisp and brown. The mulberry stalks entirely dissolve.

Serve with cream. This is greatly enjoyed.

Plum

Plums are the wonder of late summer and I look forward to them immensely. Whether you can grow them successfully depends on whether bullfinches plague you, stripping the trees not only of flower buds, which is bad enough, but of leaf buds also. Result, a snake tree with bare branches ending in a depressed tuft of leaves.

When I was young, there was no trouble from these beautiful birds. Then, a long span of forty years or so when they made plum-growing impossible. The commercial grower, of course, has to resort to trapping the blighters, but that is to make a business of what, to us, should be a pleasure.

Bullfinch populations seem to go in cycles and I am hopeful that we are now into a stretch of years when they do not bother me. Their disappearance may quite possibly correlate with the reappearance of sparrow hawks. These raptors were almost exterminated by the farmers' use of pesticides which have now been banned. Bullfinches are a favourite item in the sparrow hawk's diet. Long may the improvement last. At any rate I have taken a chance on it and replanted some plum trees.

Black plums have the most character. There's quite a bite to their flavour and it is strong. When ripe, they are excellent eaten raw, but not more, in my experience, than four at any one time, else you may have wishful regrets.

My favourite is 'Early Rivers', correctly 'Rivers' Early Prolific'. A great advantage in this variety is that, unlike most plums, it ripens so early, at the turn of July and August, that wasps are not yet a problem. But it is an uncertain cropper, meaning that it's inclined to feast or famine in alternate years. Sussex folk used to talk of there being a good shake of plums on a tree that was cropping reasonably. How that expression arose, I do not know, but certainly, with 'Early Rivers', we used to spread a sheet or two beneath, when the fruit was ripe, and simply shake the tree. When ripe, 'Early Rivers' is free-stoning, which is to say that on halving the fruit (down the groove), the stone (pit) can be removed cleanly – another tremendous advantage.

I must say a little on that most popular of all plums in Britain – 'Victoria'. It is self-pollinating and will pollinate others, such as 'Early Rivers'. Also, name two other good black plums, 'Opal' and 'Czar' – both free-stoning. 'Victoria' is

PAGES 36 AND 37 *Black 'Rivers' Early Prolific' and the luscious dusky pink of ripe 'Victoria'*

free-stoning when really ripe. Its fruits are singularly juicy and they look beautiful, with their dusky pink flush.

With us, in the south of England, it ripens in late August. This is really the only thoroughly reliable plum, even without the protection of a wall behind it, in Scotland. There, however, it will ripen a month or more later. It may not ripen at all, but can still be used.

'Victoria' is attractive but it is bland. There is little tannin in its skin. Edward Bunyard, in *The Anatomy of Dessert* (1929), wrote: 'For hungry holiday-makers fresh from school, for Bands of Hope, gatherings of the Faithful, and other charitable occasions, Victoria finds a welcome "in the raw"; but at home – to the kitchen with it.'

And hear Jane Grigson (she is speaking of the commercial grower): 'Inevitably those trees will be producing Victoria plums, and yet more Victorias, the apotheosis of a long reign is a flood of bland, boring plums. Poor Victoria. She began life in 1840, a stray seedling found in Sussex and introduced by a nurseryman in Brixton. A Cinderella story if ever there was one, except that the bridegroom was not a beautiful prince but a multi-million fruit business. Useful, comfortable, but looking for a good cropper. Victorias are for canning. Victorias are for plums and custard, that crowning moment of the school, hospital, prison and boarding house midday meal.'

I still grow 'Victoria'.

IN THE KITCHEN

If you have to pick fruit before it is ripe, you can spread it out, indoors, in front of a sunny window, for three days or so, and much of it will ripen.

While 'Bramley' apples are my staple stewed fruit for breakfast through most of the year, plums make an excellent change. For this purpose, the riper the better and quite large batches go into the freezer.

I must, however, go on to say that slightly unripe fruit is the best for obtaining a good set in jam-making. So, from any batch of fruit, I tend to sort the ripe from the unripe. The ripe I halve and then remove the pits. The pitted fruit goes into my casserole. When that is full, I add sugar – to taste, one has to say, and just enough water (only a very little) to prevent burning. Then into a low oven (150°C/300°F/gas mark 2 is about right) for 75 minutes or so. At the end of this time the fruit looks as though it's still not cooked, its shape and colour remaining perfect, but it is. I ladle it and its prolific juices into boxes and freeze them when cold. When unfrozen, they are ready to eat.

The unripe fruit goes just as it is (I seldom need to wash my own fruit, which has never been sprayed, but washing may be advisable) into a preserving pan for jam-making.

P L U M J A M

To make about 9lb of plum jam, to 6lb of plums, add less than 2½ cups of water (as little as you can get away with short of burning). Simmer (I don't mind if this takes an hour or more) so that the plums are almost a pulp. They'll set that much more easily, once the sugar is added. The simmering can go on without toughening the skins. Once the sugar is added, this is no longer the case.

Now add 1¾ cups of sugar preheated in a low oven to each 1lb of fruit. Raise the heat and boil hard, stirring often to prevent the pulp sticking. After 15 or 20 minutes,

start to test for setting. When the jam is ready, allow it to rest, off the heat, for 15 minutes. This will prevent the solid fruit from rising in the jam jars, leaving nothing but jelly at the bottom. But in any case you need, at this stage, to remove, with a spoon, as many pits as you can fish for. With a large plum, this may take only 10 or 15 minutes; with small plums or damsons, the best part of an hour. Fill the preheated jars, cover and seal. (For more detailed jam-making instructions, see pages 18–19.) Store in a cool, dark place.

P L U M A N D W A L N U T P I E

When cooking plums for friends, I like Jane's plum and walnut pie (I reduce the quantity of cinnamon).

Double quantity piecrust dough
(see page 12)
1lb plums, halved, stoned, chopped
Generous ½ cup demerara or
soft light brown sugar
1 cup walnuts, chopped
1 teaspoon ground cinnamon
Grated peel of ½ lemon and ½ orange
4 tablespoons butter, melted
Beaten egg or top-of-the-milk to glaze

Roll out the dough and use about two-thirds of it to line an 8–9in pie dish 1in deep. Leave to rest in the refrigerator or a cool place for 30 minutes.

Place a baking sheet in the oven and preheat to 180°C/350°F/gas mark 4. Mix the plums, sugar, walnuts, cinnamon and grated peel and put into the pie shell. Pour over the butter (this is not a slimline recipe). Cover with the remaining dough, pinching the edges and making a central hole. Brush over with beaten egg or top-of-the-milk. Bake for 45 minutes. Serve warm rather than hot, with cream.

Fig

F igs are just about the most luscious and exotic fruits that we in Britain can grow in our gardens, but they do need every scrap of sunshine that can be offered and their season, as also the range of varieties that can be grown, is greatly extended under glass. I am passionately fond of ripe, green figs and qualify as the archetypal fig pig.

Fig foliage does not expand till May, while a sudden and noisy leaf fall occurs in October. Still, during its brief season, it is one of the most ornamental of foliage plants available to us, and it is small wonder that Adam adopted it when obliged to hide his genitals. How he managed between October and May, history does not relate. The fig of which I write and whose leaf Adam wore, *Ficus carica*, is always deciduous, wherever it may be grown.

Many of the fig trees planted near outbuildings on large estates were chosen for their foliage rather than their fruit. Lutyens favoured 'Brunswick' for this purpose, and it is often to be found near Lutyens' houses, sometimes even when the house itself has been pulled down, as was his extension to Buckhurst Park in East Sussex. The fig survives. 'Brunswick', besides being pretty hardy, has a deeply indented, fingered leaf. It must have been Lutyens who, at Dixter, was responsible for the planting of five 'Brunswick' figs when the garden was being made, around 1911. They are still going strong and I fancy that a fig's life expectancy is indefinite. If disaster such as fire or cold overtakes the aerial parts, regeneration from basal sucker growth will enable it to perform a phoenix act.

Our other fig, probably 'Black Ischia', predates the Lloyds at Dixter, and that benefits from no protective wall or fence. I have seen the same variety at our local flower show, under the class for 'Any Other Fruit', so there must be other examples of it around my neighbourhood. I wonder when it arrived in these parts. Anyway, I have been brought up in an ethos of figs.

Figs grown in the open in our cool climate will ripen only one crop per annum. The putative fruitlets for this are carried through the previous winter, close to the tips of the previous year's young shoots. Before swelling, they are as small as or smaller than a pea, and at this stage, are relatively hardy. They start to swell at the end of April and will be destroyed overnight if there is a late frost.

Once they have survived that hazard, you may be delighted to observe how quickly they swell in May and how numerous they are. However, at the end of that month and in June, there is often a heavy fruit drop which I find hard to explain. It isn't from shortage of water, as it may happen during a late spring of high rainfall. The young shoots of the current summer will also produce young fruitlets in abundance but these, which could supply a second crop in Mediterranean-type climates, are useless in Britain. They hang on after leaf fall and should really be rubbed off at that stage, if you have the energy. This is because, as they mummify, rot works back from them into the shoot behind, and that can easily be killed. There is usually a good deal of dead wood on a fig tree at winter's end, botrytis and coral spot being the principal fungal diseases.

If we do ripen a fig crop at Dixter, 'Brunswick' will generally start in the third week of August and continue for a month. 'Black Ischia' will start only a little later, but may continue into October. 'Brunswick' is an ultra-vigorous

A 'Brunswick' fig leaf unfurls

variety and needs a good many years before maturing sufficiently to fruit. Even then, I should think we get a crop that is worth chasing up with protection against birds only one year in four. At the time of writing, I suspect that our last good crop was in 1989, because I then noted on 18th August making *Fresh Fig Tart*, from *Jane Grigson's Fruit Book*. Hear Edward Bunyard, in *The Anatomy of Dessert*, on 'Brunswick': 'a large and rather gross-looking fruit formerly known as the Madonna, but upon the arrival of George I, it was rechristened. It is not recorded if His Majesty accepted this as a compliment, but it has a certain Hanoverian lustiness, and so the name has remained.' Fruits of this variety often grow to a preposterous size, but they are good in a warm year. The trees, seen in old stable yards or on farm buildings, attain a great age and seem to thrive on neglect.

CARE AND PRUNING

Neglect, indeed, is often the best recipe for a heavy crop, because the more you prune, the more of its potential fruiting wood you are removing. But in our case and, no doubt, in many others, available space dictates that some pruning must be faced, if the tree needs to be kept into a wall. We tackle this on a serious scale one year in three, removing long, old branches that are unproductive for much of their length, and tying in younger stuff. Start with the lowest branches, each side of the central trunk, and work upwards and inwards. Never allow branches to cross over one another.

Fig trees do not require root restriction to fruit well, but if their roots are confined, they will make more manageable specimens. If you do build an underground wall to confine them, it must be remembered that summer waterings, up to the time when the fruit has reached its maximum size, will be important. Neither should feeding be neglected.

I have never grown figs under glass, but this method of cultivation, using large pots 12in or more in diameter at the mouth, enables two crops to be taken. It also opens up the possibility of growing a far wider range of varieties, many of which would not succeed outside. The pots, or other containers, should be straight-sided, so that the fig can be turned out once a year, in the dormant season. Use a strong potting compost intended for vigorous plants. When you turn the plant out of its container, rub off the soil on the outside of the ball and snip back the roots by an inch or two. Replace the fig in the same container, but work fresh compost into the outer gap. It is an awkward job (performed also for bonsai), but not difficult.

Watering should be regular (probably daily) and generous during the growing season. The idea that figs enjoy both spartan and desert conditions derives from the way one has seen them in inhospitable places where apparently wild.

Young, green 'Brunswick' figs

A fig was the last bit of vegetation I saw when I climbed Vesuvius, one blazing August day. But matters are different in cultivation, and ecological correctness can lead you astray.

PROTECTING FIGS

Figs are as popular with a range of other fauna as with ourselves. Among their most ardent seekers, in my garden, have at various times been rats and squirrels (which will eat them very green), blackbirds and starlings (two or three days before the fruit is ripe), and wasps.

There's nothing to be done against the rodents, apart from exterminating them. In town gardens, you may not be bothered by the birds. I certainly am in my garden. Wasps are a variable, from year to year. If the weather is very wet at the turn of May and June when each queen is trying to establish a new colony, wasps will be no problem later on.

Against both birds and wasps, I find it necessary to protect each fruit with a bag. Luckily the fig, unlike peaches and apricots, seems purpose-built for bag protection, but each bag must be secured, with a stem-tie, to the branch from which the fig is hanging, not around the neck of the fig itself. Even then you must be careful not to knock the fig off as you manipulate.

Fairly small plastic bags, into which holes are punched at regular intervals, are suitable. I use what are known as lettuce bags, which are of this kind. But because, even with the holes, the fig generates a moist atmosphere within them, the bags should not be fitted a day before necessary, or you're more likely to end up with a rotten than a ripe fruit. Just as the fruit is beginning to colour from pure green to something a little warmer is the moment for bagging up, and that, in fine weather, will be exactly three days prior to the ripe fruit being ready for you. So, if the crop warrants all the exercise and ladder work, I go through the figs every third day, removing bags from ripe fruits and reusing them on those that will shortly ripen. If you can get a fig enthusiast to do this job for you, so much the better. It is difficult to eat more than three large figs in a day, so that will leave plenty over.

The fruit of 'Brunswick' is green on the shaded side but deep, warm brown where the sun has touched it, and it is pear-shaped. When ripe, the skin will split longitudinally in several places. It is an invariable signal, and the fruit is

'Brunswick' figs, nearly ripe

44

never ready for picking before this. It does not ripen off the tree, so premature harvesting never pays. An unripe fig has nothing to recommend it.

'Black Ischia' has a much darker fruit, smaller and with a long, narrow neck. Again it splits on ripening and the interior is crimson red. It has more flavour than 'Brunswick' but is less juicy. 'Brown Turkey' is the most widely grown hardy fig. The squat little dark-blue-skinned figs that reach us from Turkey in the autumn are simply called black figs by the Turks.

EATING FIGS

There is no more sumptuous sight than a large, dish-shaped bowl, brimming with ripe figs. The skin at the stalk-end of the fruit is rather thick, and should be discarded. At the bulbous end, however, it is thin and can be ignored. So the simplest way to eat a raw fig is by peeling it like a banana. Eat it from the broadly pointed top downwards, ignoring the skin as you reach the 'eye'. This is a messy performance, requiring a final licking of the fingers, but that is part of the enjoyment.

BAKED FIGS

My godson Michael Schuster and Monika, his wife, picked this up from somewhere and passed it on to me, as a willing recipient. Usually it will be made with Turkish black figs, which sit comfortably on their bottoms. With the elongated figs that I grow, it is only necessary to make incisions on the side of each fig that will lie underneath. Two figs per person, even of the black Turkish kind, should be ample, though the recipe recommends four. So adjust the recommendation for sixteen figs for four people according to their appetites and the size of the figs used.

16 black Turkish or other fresh figs
1 cup *crème fraîche* or sour cream *or*
a half-and-half mixture of the two
1–4 tablespoons confectioners' sugar

1 tablespoon orange liqueur, or other
fruit or nut liqueur
Large mint leaf

Optional
Small handful of red berry fruit to garnish
Shortbread, or similar, cookies to serve

Preheat the oven to 180°C/350°F/gas mark 4. Lightly butter a baking pan.

Cut the stems off the figs. In the case of the black Turkish variety, cut a ¼in deep cross in their blossom end. In the case of elongated figs, make one small, lengthways incision. Arrange the figs, cut-side down, in the buttered pan. Bake them, uncovered, for 30 minutes or until they start to collapse. Let them cool.

Transfer the fig juices to a bowl and

blend them with the remaining ingredients. Spoon enough of this sauce on to each of 4 plates to make a pool about 4in across. Place the figs on top of the sauce and gar- nish with a mint leaf. Add a few berries to the plate, if available. (There should be autumn-fruiting raspberries around.) A crisp cookie makes a good garnish, too.

MARINATED FIGS

A recipe given to me by my friend Chloë Carr, during a glut. Serves 4 to 6.

12 large ripe figs
2 tablespoons superfine sugar
About 4 tablespoons brandy
1¼ cups heavy cream
1 tablespoon finely grated semisweet chocolate

Cut the figs in quarters and arrange them in a dish, preferably in a single layer. Sprinkle over the sugar, then the brandy. Cover and leave to marinate at room temperature for several hours.

Just before serving, whip the cream to soft peaks and fold it into the figs. Transfer to a serving dish and scatter the grated chocolate on top.

FRESH FIG TART

A French way of presenting fresh figs, given in *Jane Grigson's Fruit Book* and described by her as most attractive to look at, as well as good to eat.

1lb fresh figs
3–4 tablespoons orange liqueur
3 tablespoons apricot jam

Sweet pastry dough
1 stick butter, soft but cool
2 rounded tablespoons vanilla sugar
1 extra-large egg
Pinch of salt
2 cups all-purpose flour

Rinse and dry the figs. If the skins are tough, peel them away. Halve the figs and put them on a plate. Pour over the orange liqueur and cover with plastic wrap. Leave in the refrigerator for several hours to macerate.

For the pastry dough, cream the butter and sugar, then add the egg and salt. When the mixture is well amalgamated, add the flour. Put the dough in a plastic bag and rest in the refrigerator or a cool place for at least 30 minutes.

Roll out the dough to line an 8in tart pan (see page 21). Leave to rest again for 30 minutes to an hour. Place a baking sheet in the oven and preheat to 180°C/350°F/gas mark 4. Pre-bake for about 20 minutes, until the tart shell is completely cooked, but barely coloured.

Heat the apricot jam gently and sieve it into a small bowl. Mix in the liquid from the figs. Put the fig halves on the tart shell, as decoratively as you can. Spoon over them the apricot and orange mixture. Put in the refrigerator to chill.

Pear

The special quality of pears as we most appreciate them was well expressed by Edward Bunyard in *The Anatomy of Dessert*: 'As it is, in my view, the duty of an apple to be crisp and crunchable, a pear should have such a texture as leads to silent consumption, and I therefore exclude from my pages all those notoriously crisp and glassy in flesh. Among the thousands of pears which exist it is easy to avoid those primitive varieties which have not learned the art of being fondant.'

Most pears should be peeled before being eaten raw, although there is a satisfaction in approaching the long, thin calabash type, such as 'Conference', from the top and devouring rounds of it downwards, until the core is reached and a more lateral approach becomes necessary. But the peeling of a pear is in itself a satisfaction, as is dealing, or failing to deal, with the coy slipperiness of the undressed fruit. Juice everywhere. How does one cope with it? The very helplessness of a pear devotee is a part of his thrall.

Edwardian walled gardens were stuffed with espalier and cordon pear trees, basking against a southerly aspect. Northwest would be reserved for a cooking pear, probably of slow maturation, but excellent when stewed over a long period, while the initially anaemic white colouring changed gradually to rich, rosy brown. There is a huge such espalier of an unnamed cooker against Lutyens' chimney breast at the northwest end of Dixter, and it makes a striking appendage noticed by all visitors. 'That must be terribly old,' one such, a lady, said to me. 'How old are you?' I dared to ask. 'I was seventy-five last week,' said she proudly. 'Well, that's just about the age of the pear. You don't feel terribly old, do you?' And she didn't.

But there were pear trees at Dixter before the Lloyds' arrival in 1910. Two of them still exist, in an excellent state of health, in so far as that is possible without any spraying. One is a 'Williams', and that is a martyr to scab, if the early summer weather is wet and the infection occurs early. The fruits become blotched and malshapen, cracking open on the infected areas. But that does not happen, seriously, in every year and the flavour is amazingly sweet and strong (and musky), compared with anything the shops have to offer. It isn't starved, either, as it grows in a plot where we line out vegetables and plants

'Williams' pears on the old tree that predates the arrival of the Lloyds at Dixter

48

and that is regularly manured. Pears are greedy.

These two old pears were grafted on wild pear seedlings, which was invariably the practice at that time. Pear stock gives rise to a large and vigorous tree, whether you want that or not. Nowadays, quince is used in preference, and the scion is of a more manageable and predictable size. Our 'Doyenné du Comice' espaliers were replanted in the 1930s and are all on quince stock. These espaliers, which line the backs of flower borders in a part of the garden originally designated, in the main, for the growing of vegetables (the pears formed a screen between the flowers next to the paths and the vegetable plots behind them – the customary Edwardian arrangement) are full of character, being gnarled and covered with lichens, though not good examples of the way fruit should be grown. They need a pollinator and the 'Williams' is near enough to serve them. They do crop, though not heavily, and I pick them as late as I dare, usually at the end of September, sometimes later. It depends on how swiftly the birds set about them.

STORING PEARS

Ideally, you should not pick pears until, when you lift a fruit that is hanging on the branch, it parts easily at the natural callus between fruit stalk and tree. However, all pears are picked unripe, being too vulnerable to wind and predators if left on the tree. Our pears are nowadays stored in my roomy larder, each fruit given a ventilated plastic lettuce bag to itself. This prevents shrivelling before the fruit is ripe. It is important that no fruit should be touching its neighbour. Then, if any should rot, the rot will not spread. The bag treatment sees to this and works well for slow-maturing apples, too.

Telling whether a pear is ripe is always a problem, even when you are experienced. The signs differ between varieties and between fruits within the same variety. The colour of a pear changes as ripeness approaches, but this can be deceptive. A sleepy pear may still have green in the skin, which seems unfair. My father used to place both thumbs alongside each other and not quite touching, right at the top of the fruit, and then draw them inwards towards each other. If the skin wrinkled, then the fruit was ripe. I still use this method but it works only if the fruit hasn't shrivelled at all.

With us, the fruit of 'Comice' ripens in November, but not all at once. You need to be vigilant. 'Williams' ripens late in September and needs only two or three weeks between picking and eating. Late-maturing pears, like 'Olivier de

The lichen-covered 'Doyenné du Comice' espaliers dating from the early 1930s

Serres' and 'Winter Nelis', picked just before the birds start attacking them and properly stored, will see you well into February.

If you don't grow your own, the most likely place to find ripe pears is an old-fashioned greengrocer's. Make sure you choose your own. You will rarely buy a pear that's already ripe in a supermarket; shelf life wouldn't allow that. Neither would the appallingly rough handling that you witness, first by staff, chucking the goods into their selling trays, and later by the public, who don't scruple to bang their thumbs into almost every fruit on view.

51

IN THE KITCHEN

If cooking unripe pears, it often helps to stew them for a short while in a very little water, before getting on with your recipe.

PEARS IN SYRUP

Two versions of the same recipe, both from Jane Grigson's *English Food.*

Version 1
6 pears, peeled, cored and halved
Red wine (inexpensive will do)
Sugar

1 stick cinnamon
Pinch of ground ginger

Place the pears in a pan in a single layer, and pour in enough red wine to cover them. Add 2 tablespoons sugar, the cinnamon and the ginger. Cover and simmer until the pears are done.

ABOVE *The branches of the spur-pruned espalier gleam in winter sun*
RIGHT *'Comice' pears on the gnarled espalier*

52

Using a perforated spoon, remove them to a dish and keep them hot. Boil down their cooking liquid until it is slightly syrupy. Taste it from time to time, and put in more sugar if you like – the flavour should be fairly strong and sweet, but not over-sweet. Pour, boiling, over the pears and leave to cool. Don't strain out the cinnamon stick; it adds to the appearance, as well as the flavour, of the dish.

Version 2

If quinces are available, I even prefer this recipe. Should wine be out of the question (is it ever?), add three sliced quinces to the six halved pears and substitute a vanilla bean, split, for the cinnamon stick. Cover with water, and start with 4 tablespoons of sugar. If you cook the dish slowly enough, the juice will turn a most beautiful deep red.

PEAR TART

From *Jane Grigson's Fruit Book* and will serve 8 (6 if greedy).

4 or 5 ripe pears
1 tablespoon lemon juice
1¼ cups heavy or whipping cream
2 extra-large egg yolks
Vanilla sugar

Sweet pastry dough
1 stick butter, soft but cool
2 tablespoons vanilla sugar
1 extra-large egg
Pinch of salt
2½ cups all-purpose flour

Make the pastry dough: cream the butter and sugar; add the egg and salt; when well amalgamated, add the flour. Put in a plastic bag and rest in the refrigerator or a cool place for 30 minutes.

Roll out the dough to line a large tart pan, 10in diameter or slightly larger (see page 21). Leave to rest again, for 30 minutes to an hour. Place a baking sheet in the oven and preheat to 190°C/375°F/gas mark 5. Pre-bake the tart shell until it is very lightly coloured, about 15 minutes.

Meanwhile, peel, core and halve the pears, keeping the halves in shape. Sprinkle with, or turn in, lemon juice, to prevent discolouring. Beat together the cream and egg yolks, sweetening to taste with vanilla sugar.

When the pastry comes out of the oven, arrange the pear halves on it, spreading them out slightly so that they are flattened but still in the shape of halves, with the pointed ends towards the centre. Pour over the cream mixture and return to the oven. Close the door and turn the heat down to 180°C/350°F/gas mark 4. Bake till the cream is nearly firm. It tastes best when not quite set in the centre. Serve warm.

Note: Should your pears be on the hard side, first stew them gently in a little syrup with lemon juice and lemon peel. Eating apples can also be used for this tart. It is a good idea to cook the slices in a little butter first, so they begin to soften.

PEAR AND ALMOND CRUMBLE

The same recipe as for *Apricot and Almond Crumble* (page 20), but the pears, unless very ripe, should first be stewed in a little water with the sugar.

PEAR UPSIDE-DOWN CAKE FLAVOURED WITH GINGER

In *Jane Grigson's Fruit Book*, this is called *Springfield Pear Cake*. She recommends making it in a shallow cake pan, but I find an oval gratin dish (as she recommends for pineapple upside-down cake) better: the cake is less likely to stick when it is turned upside down. A 7 x 11in dish works out right.

Preserved ginger comes expensive if purchased in fancy jars, as one normally sees it. I buy it by the gallon. It is so good on its own, with cream, or, better still, with the further addition of banana sliced into it. And it has frequent culinary uses. Unfortunately, there will always be a proportion of your friends who cannot abide ginger. I couldn't as a child, but grew out of that. Surely one should adapt, unless made physically uncomfortable by the food in question.

Cake
1 stick butter, softened
Generous ½ cup sugar
¾ cup self-rising flour
1 level teaspoon baking powder
¼ cup finely ground blanched almonds
2 extra-large eggs
3–4 tablespoons syrup from
preserved ginger
4 knobs preserved ginger,
coarsely chopped

Topping
6 tablespoons salted butter, cut up
Scant ½ cup sugar
2 tablespoons preserved ginger syrup
3–6 firm pears
Juice of 1 lemon

To make the topping, melt together the butter, sugar and syrup. Pour over the base of the gratin dish. Brush the mixture up the sides and let it fall back.

Peel, core and thinly slice the pears, turning them in lemon juice so that they do not discolour. Arrange them in an attractive pattern on the toffee base.

Tip all the cake ingredients, except the chopped ginger, into the bowl of an electric mixer or food processor, and whizz to smoothness. Or beat everything vigorously together with a wooden spoon. Add the ginger and spread over the top of the pears. Bake in an oven preheated to 150°C/300°F/gas mark 2 and take a look after 50 minutes. Leave till the cake is golden brown and has slightly contracted from the edge. A skewer pushed in almost horizontally should come out clean. Leave to cool for a few minutes on a wire rack, then run a broad knife blade between the dish and the edge of the cake to make sure there are no sticking patches.

Put a rimmed serving plate on top, upside-down, then turn the whole thing as rapidly as possible – use a cloth to protect your hands. A certain amount of juice will flow from the cake, but this only adds to its deliciousness.

Serve hot, warm or cold, on its own, or with cream as a pudding. It's a spoon-and-fork cake, being far too messy to eat with your fingers.

Apple

*R*aw apples should form an everyday part of one's diet. 'Cox' is the king and is readily available in commerce. Long may that last. There are many other interesting aromatic, textured and flavoured apples but they appear on the market with increasing rarity, being 'uncommercial'. That means that we need to grow them ourselves. Luckily, there are still nurseries that specialize in uneconomic varieties from whom we can buy the young trees or bushes. To assist you in your choice, I include below notes on a dozen dessert apples, mainly reprinted from an article published by the Royal Horticultural Society in *The Garden*, September 1981, wherein I described some fifty varieties of dessert apple that I'd tasted over the previous two years.

There used to be many different apples growing at Dixter, but for various reasons I gradually gave them up. For one thing, our heavy soil makes them susceptible to apple canker disease. Then there was the orchard/meadow factor. The chief importance of my meadow areas to me is the wide variety of plants naturalized in them. To be successful, this largely depends on a low nutrient status in the soil. If the ground is fertile, this will benefit coarse herbage at the expense of the most interesting flora. Yet a low nutrient status doesn't suit the fruit trees. Their fruit tends to be small, hard and woody. Then, certain apples (not 'Bramley') were regularly disbudded by bullfinches. However, as I have mentioned under plums (see page 35), this bird now seems to be considerably down in numbers and I have not seen it in my garden for five years.

The last of our old apple trees blew over in the storms of October 1987 and January 1990 (we had to help a few of them on their way). A number of them were anyway already suffering from honey fungus, *Armillaria mellea*. We traced their roots conscientiously and dug them out. Those missed gave away their presence when fructifications appeared on the surface in the following autumns. This enabled us to locate remaining infections and to dig out the residual roots.

Picking up my courage, I have now done a little replanting, taking care not to plant an apple where there was an apple before, since apples, like roses,

A crab apple, Malus hupehensis, *blossoms among the naturalized plants in the old orchard. This ornamental crab was grown from a pip*

are liable to replant disease and do not thrive on the site where an apple grew before. This was not a problem as the orchard was mixed, including pears and plums. I planted 'Red Miller's Seedling', 'Sunset', 'Orléans Reinette' and 'St Everard' (see below).

I have not replanted 'Bramley's Seedling'. This was and remains my mainstay for culinary purposes, but its fruit is easily come by. On the whole I am glad I no longer grow it. True, it makes an imposingly large tree and is a picture in the first week of May, the blossom being a definite shade of pink. But in some years, one in three, perhaps, it would fail to flower or fruit. And the fruit is liable to a physiological deficiency disease (of magnesium, I believe), called bitter pit. It causes brown spotting right through the flesh, although virtually invisible on the surface. You'll often find this trouble in fruit you have bought, especially on the largest specimens.

Nor have I replanted 'Blenheim Orange'. This was highly esteemed by my father, who planted a great many at Dixter; as also by Edward Bunyard, who wrote in *The Anatomy of Dessert*, 'The man who cannot appreciate a Blenheim has not come to years of gustatory discretion; he probably drinks sparkling Muscatelle. There is in this noble fruit a mellow austerity as of a great port in its prime . . . ' Mellow, yes; austere, not in the least. Old woolly pants would be my nickname for this apple, which at Dixter remained in a typical overripe condition from November to March. It is an overlarge fruit anyway; most pleasing, I find, if caught in October before it is quite ripe but is still juicy rather than woolly.

DESSERT APPLES

ASHMEAD'S KERNEL Fairly small, flattish, hard-looking; dusky scurf with small red flush on sunny side. Not as hard as it looks. Crumbles well in mouth. White flesh. Rather nutty but not excessively so. Sweet enough but neither cloying nor aromatic. Could be eaten in quantity.

DISCOVERY ('Worcester Pearmain' x 'Beauty of Bath') Flattened globe. Nice skin, yellow with red flush. Pleasant aroma. Flesh firm and crisp. Flavour oversweet and perfumed, too much so for extended eating.

EGREMONT RUSSET Rough, rusty exterior. Flesh solid, hard. Curious musty flavour, all right if you like that sort of personality. Quite juicy but with a dry finish on the tongue. I tire of this apple very quickly.

FIESTA ('Cox' × 'Idared') Bred at East Malling. Crosses with 'Cox' as one parent are always comparing themselves to that famous apple, but to their own advantage. 'Fiesta' is said to crop twice as heavily as 'Cox'. So what?, since it both looks different and has no 'Cox' flavour. It is a good dessert apple in its own right. Midseason, but storing well. Of fair size, somewhat flattened, small eye. Colour, a mix of yellow with quite a bit of red flush. Little aroma (an easily overdone quality) and not waxy. Crisp, with a fresh (not cloying) flavour and plenty of juice. Sweet but with just enough acidity. Not wildly exciting, even so.

GALA ('Kidd's Orange Red' × 'Golden Delicious') In the south of England ripens in November but keeps well barn-stored till March. From New Zealand. Nice shape, neither long nor squat but with bumpy shoulders. Yellow dappled fairly evenly with red. Not bright but cheerful. Quite hard, crisp, very juicy with slight but pleasing aroma. Warm and pleasing flavour though not much of it. Main virtues: juice and scrunch. Needs a little more acidity. Good with cheese.

GOLDEN DELICIOUS Parentage in doubt. Yellow skin spotted and streaked in home-grown specimens with ugly brown scurf. Exactly the right resistance and crispness when bitten into. Fresh, juicy sweet, but not too sweet, a little pleasing flavour but only a little and minimal aroma. Could become an addiction. It doesn't cloy so that you're always ready for the next. (I'm sorry I couldn't be more beastly about this aggressive monster.)

GREENSLEEVES ('James Grieve' × 'Golden Delicious') Nice size and globular shape, green or yellow-green all over. Should be eaten young when still firm and a little acid. A bit insipid even then but fresh, not soft and cloying as later, when there will be no compensations for an overall shortage on personality.

JAMES GRIEVE ('Potts' Seedling' ×) Rounded, waxy, soft and easily bruised. Basically green but can flush on sunny side. Juicy, slightly acid and refreshing but sweet enough and pleasantly flavoured. Should be kept until flavour develops. This is my favourite forerunner to 'Cox', but hear Bunyard: 'This is one of the very few apples resulting from the marriage of a cooking and a dessert apple which is of dessert quality. One feels that, like some of the recently ennobled we know of, it is a near thing, and untoward circumstances such as a cold and sunless summer reveal the humbler origin. But given a fair chance we welcome the newcomer, thankful for the melting, almost marrowy flesh, abundant juice and fragrant aroma.'

MERTON WORCESTER ('Cox' × 'Worcester Pearmain') and 'WORCESTER PEARMAIN' ('Devonshire Quarrenden' ×) Tried concurrently because so similar in appearance. Broadly conical, small eye, heavy red flush on three-quarters of surface. Firm, crisp white flesh. Little aroma. 'Merton Worcester' has an extra sharpness that is welcome and makes it easier to finish eating. Pleasantly chewy but still not much of an apple. 'Worcester Pearmain' is sweeter, more insipid. The first bite is always the best.

ORLEANS REINETTE Very like 'Blenheim' in appearance with same open eye. Quite different aroma and not so woolly. Flesh firm. Very agreeable flavour without being insistent; one could eat a number in a row. With its dry finish and flavour, has much in common with the russets.

RED MILLER'S SEEDLING Large, red, waxy. ('Miller's Seedling' differs only in colour: pale yellow with interrupted flush on sunny side.) Brisk, fresh, crisp, juicy. Mild-flavoured, not perfumed. An excellent eat in its early season, albeit watery.

SUNSET Too small to be commercial, but suits me. Flattened globe, smooth, flushed red on one side. Crisp and juicy. Fresh fruity flavour, not cloying.

IN THE KITCHEN

Jane Grigson did not think highly of 'Bramley', and I can quite see why. It retains no shape when cooked and rises into an undifferentiated froth. This, together with its acidity, is one of the reasons for my liking it as stewed apple on my breakfast table. It is a feature of breakfast at Dixter almost year round that many of my guests both expect and appreciate.

STEWED APPLES

I peel, core and slice the apples into a stew pan, add a lot of sugar (too much, for some of my friends, but I don't eat it with cream as well) and the minimum of water. This varies with the state of the fruit. If hard and dry, more water will be required. If soft and juicy, only a few tablespoons. I place the covered pan on a hottish setting and set the timer for 13 to 15 minutes. By then the fruit should have cooked right through so that all you see is a frothy mass, rapidly rising, if you're not prompt, to overflow and make a nasty mess on the stove. Don't ignore the timer's signal.

APPLESAUCE

Stewed 'Bramley' makes the perfect basis for applesauce, to accompany roast pork.

Melt 2 tablespoons butter in a pan and slowly cook, covered, a finely chopped onion together with some (not too much – you must be the judge) chopped common sage. Add seasoning and about 2 cups stewed apple, which should be in a puréed condition. Serve hot.

NORMANDY PHEASANT

An excellent recipe given by Jane Grigson in both *Good Things* and the *Fruit Book*. Chicken can be cooked in the same way. Serves 3 to 4.

1 large oven-ready pheasant
6 tablespoons butter
6 medium-sized 'Reinette' or 'Cox', peeled, cored, sliced
Ground cinnamon
½ cup heavy cream
4 tablespoons Calvados (or, if unavailable, single malt whisky)
Salt, pepper

In a flameproof casserole, brown the pheasant in half the butter. In the remaining butter, fry the apple slices in a skillet, sprinkling them with cinnamon as they cook.

Remove the pheasant and make a layer of apple at the base of the casserole, replace the bird and tuck the remaining apple slices around it. Pour in half the cream, over the bird and apples. Cover and cook at 180°C/350°F/gas mark 4 for about an hour.

Remove the casserole and turn the oven heat up to 230°C/450°F/gas mark 8. Meantime, pour the remaining cream over the pheasant, then add the Calvados or whisky. Check the seasoning. Cover and return to the oven for 5 minutes. Serve from the casserole.

DANISH PUDDING

This was one of my mother's favourite recipes and it continues to be as popular with my friends. Why Danish, I do not know. It came to my mother from Mrs Sinden, who cooked for us at one time.

4–5 medium-sized apples, peeled, cored and sliced, and lightly pre-cooked (unless using 'Bramley', when pre-cooking is unnecessary)
1 generous cup dates, chopped
Up to 1¼ cups heavy or whipping cream, whipped
Few split almonds, toasted lightly in the oven

Almond paste
1 cup finely ground blanched almonds
½ cup confectioners' sugar
Yolks of 2 eggs

Meringue
½ cup superfine or granulated sugar
Whites of 2 eggs, stiffly beaten

Line the bottom of a deep, oval baking dish with the slices of apple. Add a layer of chopped dates.

Mix the ground almonds and confectioners' sugar with the yolks of 2 eggs to the consistency of a soft paste. Spread in a layer over the dates and bake in a preheated oven at 150°C/300°F/gas mark 2 for 15 minutes.

Fold the superfine or granulated sugar lightly into the stiffly beaten egg whites and cover the almond paste with this meringue. Bake at the same temperature for 30 minutes.

When cold, cover with whipped cream and garnish with the toasted split almonds.

Actually, my mother garnished with candied cherries, which are such a pretty colour. I adored them as a child and she sent me huge Madeira cakes to school, each containing 122 cherries (she counted everything, as I do). However, Jane Grigson is, I'm sure rightly, so disdainful of these tasteless cherries that I have switched to almonds.

APPLE CHARLOTTE

With a recipe that you do infrequently, it is a great help to be writing about it, as in this case, soon after the event. I had been given some large 'Blenheim Orange' apples and wanted a good use for them at a dinner. Any well-flavoured dessert apple would do. As so often, I followed Jane Grigson, but found that I needed even more than the 1½ sticks of butter she stipulates, as bread is magnificently absorbent.

1½lb apples, peeled, cored and sliced
2 sticks butter
Generous ½–¾ cup superfine or
granulated sugar
1 or 2 egg yolks (optional)
Medium-thin sliced loaf of white or
soft-grain bread, crusts removed

The apples can be cooked in advance. Put a knob of butter into a heavy pan with just enough water to cover the base thinly. Add the fruit to the pan and stir in a generous ½ cup of sugar. Cover and cook gently until the juices run, then more vigorously without a lid, so that the apples cook to as unwatery a pulp as possible (hence 'Bramley' would be unsuitable).

Off the heat, stir in the egg yolk, which helps to cohere the pulp slightly, though it is not absolutely necessary.

Cut the remaining butter into cubes. Bring to the boil in a small pan, stirring. When the white salty crust separates from the yellow oil, pour through a damp cloth-lined strainer into a dish. Brush some of the clarified butter over a metal cake or bread pan, approximately 5 cup capacity. Put in a heaped tablespoon of sugar and turn the pan about, so that it is completely coated inside.

Cut pieces of bread, 1½in wide, to the height of the pan. Dip both sides into the butter and press gently into place against the side of the pan. Leave no gaps. Cut a large piece for the base, dip that in butter and lay on the bottom. Brush all joints with lightly beaten egg white, to strengthen the palisade. Cut another piece of bread for the lid, dip in butter, too, then set aside.

Fill the cavity with apple pulp, tepid or cold rather than hot. Put the bread lid on top. (It doesn't matter if the edges of bread and lid come slightly above the top of the pan.)

Bake for about an hour in a preheated oven at 190°C/375°F/gas mark 5, until nicely and richly browned. Should it be ready before you get to the pudding stage, apple charlotte will keep warm happily at a lower heat. To serve, run a knife round the inside of the pan, then invert a warm plate on top and turn the whole thing over rapidly. Superfine or granulated sugar and a jug of the best cream set apple charlotte off perfectly.

Another classic apple dish is *Blackberry and Apple Pie*, given on page 99.

Quince

*I*t is the true quince, *Cydonia oblonga*, that I write of, not the Japanese quince or 'japonica' (various species of *Chaenomeles*), that we grow as ornamental flowering shrubs. These do fruit, but for culinary purposes have little flavour.

The quince really enjoys more heat than we can give it in Britain, but will crop well in good years. Even in northwest Scotland, there are quinces at Dundonnell which occasionally manage to fruit, and they are not against a wall. In the chilly north, were you serious about obtaining fruit, a warm south-facing wall would be the better siting.

The quince is a long-lived tree and it has for centuries been recognized that it likes moist places. It was frequently planted on pond margins. At Dixter,

The quince makes an unruly, though picturesque, tree or large bush

there were two, each side of a pond, close to the house, into which the sewage drained (before the Lloyd family's arrival in 1910). The pond was drained and the quinces died. But we still have one old one, in a wet spot by the rubbish heap at the bottom of our orchard. From time to time, it crops usefully, but more often than not is bedevilled by leaf blight, a fungal disease which shows up as reddish-brown spots on leaves and fruit. In wet springs, this entirely defoliates the tree and a second crop of leaves is put forth. Putative fruits just disappear.

Flowering, however, is always abundant and quinces are self-pollinating. The flowers are charming, quite large, borne singly, soft pink and set among the pale, furry young leaves. As soon as faded, we should spray with a protective fungicide. Perhaps, now that my memory has been jogged, we might get around to it next May, but it is January as I write and it's still a long time ahead. So much needs doing in May.

Pick the mature, fresh fruit as late as you dare, but watch out for the depredations of brown rot fungal patches. I generally find it advisable to use the quinces up fairly quickly, in several of various ways. The experts warn that quinces, whose aroma is extremely strong and personal (one fruit is enough to scent a room), should never be stored near to apples or pears, whose flavour will be affected. This might, surely, be a subtle way of introducing the quince flavour, which goes so well with both apples and pears, without actually having to use the quince! For any apple or pear pie or tart, the addition of a small amount of quince will greatly enhance the flavour; but it must not be overdone, or the principal flavour will be drowned.

A quince tree loaded with ripe fruits is a wonderful sight, as they are luminous yellow and glow in October sunshine. You can pick out the trees as you drive around the countryside. 'The quince is a tree to look out for in other people's gardens, in case they do not appreciate it, or are willing to share its fruit,' wrote Jane Grigson, in the *Fruit Book*. This was also my mother's principle. And she spotted a quince tree in a cottager's front garden in Beckley, the next village to ours. We passed it to and from Rye, on Monday afternoons, when my sister and I were taken to the dancing class (I did not enjoy those occasions). Once a year, on our way home, we would stop at that cottage and my mother would buy the crop.

PAGES 64–65 *From bud to yellow-gold fruit*
RIGHT *Ripe quinces hang on the tree*

She turned it into crystallized quince or *Quittenpaste*, a German recipe which she collected in Frankfurt am Main. 'Paste', pronounced in a Continental way, is quite an acceptable word. 'Home paste' or 'house paste' is hardly an alternative to *pâté maison* either. This sweetmeat was to be eaten at the end of a meal. One of its attractions was the shape of the metal moulds into which the liquid quince was poured. These, also, were acquired in Frankfurt, where my mother much preferred to buy all her kitchen utensils (Staines, in Victoria Street, London, was the only possible alternative).

QUITTENPASTE

Tante Luise's recipe

Take 5 large apple quinces (these are better than the pear-shaped ones) and two large apples, peel them and boil until they are tender. Then take them out of the water and pass through a wire sieve.

[After peeling and coring: 1lb of apple to 2lb of quince.]

To every pound and a half of fruit, add 1¼lb of sugar. When the fruit is passed through the sieve and the sugar added, boil again for 10 minutes or more until it begins to thicken, but it must not get too thick. The preserve must be stirred all the time it is boiling with a wooden spoon. Have a pan of boiling water ready on the table and stand the preserving pan in it to keep the *paste hot whilst filling the moulds. A silver spoon should be used to keep the fruit a good colour.*

When the preserve had set, it was turned out of the moulds on to wire trays on a deep, sunny window sill, between the day and night nurseries, there remaining until a crystallized crustiness formed on the surface. This did not always happen. I think a warm airing cupboard would have been better. Sunny the window sill might be, but in late autumn there's not much sun.

Quittenpaste is so dense, the flavour so concentrated, that only a very little can be eaten at a time.

QUINCE PULP

Any quince that is left over from immediate kitchen uses can be cooked, strained, sweetened (but not too much), and then stored as pulp in small boxes in the deep-freeze. It is wonderful to have a supply to draw on at any time of the year.

QUINCE JAM

One immediate use to which I put quinces is the making of jam. The chunkiness of jam gives it a rough texture, which the quince cheese that my mother also made, adding sugar to strained quince pulp, notably lacked. That was of far too dense and uniform a texture. It was a correspondent from Essex, Mr Boys Smith, who pointed out to me that quinces do not need to be peeled, and I have never, for any purpose, done so since. On cooking, the skins simply melt away. Quartering and coring the fruit (the core is large and the pips are arranged in serried ranks) is all that's necessary.

Weigh your fruit (about 6lb is a good quantity, making about 10lb jam); quarter and core it, tip into a preserving pan and add 2½ cups of water to each 2lb of fruit. Simmer till the fruit is perfectly soft and the water much reduced – not more than an hour. Add 2½ cups sugar (preheated in the oven) for each 1lb of fruit. Boil fast till setting point is reached. Remove the jam from the stove and allow it to stand for 15 minutes before pouring it into preheated jars and sealing (see page 19). Store in a cool, dark place.

CHICKEN STEW WITH QUINCE

From Jane Grigson's *Good Things,* in my battered old copy of which I made the marginal comment, 'so good and easy'. Serves 4 to 6.

1 large chicken, jointed
1 stick butter
2 large onions, finely chopped
Bunch of parsley, chopped
About ½ teaspoon ground ginger
Salt, black cayenne (my cayenne is red)
and paprika pepper
1lb quinces (or more to taste)

The chicken pieces are not browned before cooking. Put them and 2 tablespoons of the butter into a large pan with the onions and parsley. Just cover with cold water and season with ginger, salt and the peppers. Bring to the boil and simmer for about an hour, until the chicken is tender and, when it is pierced with the tip of a knife, the juices run clear.

Slice and core the quinces (leave the peel on), then brown them very lightly in the remaining butter. Add to the stew half an hour before the end of cooking.

AN EIGHTEENTH-CENTURY QUINCE PUDDING

For this I often turn to quince pulp stored in the freezer (see opposite). The recipe is from Jane Grigson's *Good Things.* Serves 6.

1¼ cups cream (heavy, light or a mixture)
2 egg yolks
⅔ cup quince purée
Sugar
Ground ginger
4 tablespoons butter, diced

Beat the cream with the egg yolks and add the quince purée. Add sugar and ginger to taste. Stir the butter into the mixture.

Butter a baking dish and pour in the quince mixture. Bake in a preheated oven at 160°C/325°F/gas mark 3, or less, until set. Eat hot. As this pudding is a kind of fruit custard, it's important not to cook it so fast that the mixture boils – this will curdle the eggs. The proportion of fruit purée to custard may be varied to taste. The purée should be on the dry side, not in the least sloppy.

Medlar

Y ou could scarcely choose a prettier small tree for the garden than the medlar, *Mespilus germanica*. Its culinary properties might not be a primary reason for wanting one, but it has many other charms. The spreading habit, with branches down to the ground (if you allow this) is one, and the characteristic, scaly-barked trunk. Large white flowers are borne, singly, in May. In autumn, the leaves never fail to colour to a warm orange-brown and the fruits, which ripen after leaf fall, are amazingly individual: globular, brown, of a somewhat roughened texture and with a huge 'eye', framed by a ruff of persistent sepals.

Medlars are always grafted, usually on wild hawthorn, which is an unfortunate choice. It will always end up by suckering and hawthorn suckers are neither pretty nor pleasant to handle. Both medlars that we have grown at Dixter were worked on hawthorn. In the first case, the hawthorn stock was run up to 5ft and worked high, so that the trunk was hawthorn, not medlar – a great deprivation. I like hawthorn trunks but prefer them crowned by hawthorn. This tree was always weakly and eventually died.

The second is still alive and vigorous, after some forty-five years. Here, the hawthorn graft was made at ground level, so the medlar has its own trunk. Quince is also used as a stock and, if you have the choice, go for that.

MEDLAR JELLY

Medlar jelly is sharp and suitable to go with game and other strong meats. Use the fruit when nearly ripe but before it has gone soft and bletted. The word 'bletted' is only used of medlars and describes the soft, over-ripe condition that has to be reached – in late autumn – before they are edible raw. Don't bother, is my advice, unless you wish to be known as a connoisseur; but you might, equally, be mistaken for a poseur.

Cut the fruit into quarters; stew gently with enough water not quite to cover the fruit in the pan; then allow to drip, overnight, through a jelly bag. Jelly bags tend to look like upturned pixie hats. Mine is made of thick felt, but nowadays they are more often made of nylon. The bag is scalded with boiling water, so that the juice will flow freely through it, and then suspended by its four lugs over a mixing bowl into which the juice drips. We have our own Heath Robinson device. Some people harness an upturned four-legged stool.

Measure the juice and allow 2½ cups of sugar (preheated in the oven) to 2½ cups

Our medlar in flower, in May

of juice. If the juice was not thick and glutinous before heating, I recommend boiling it for a while, to concentrate it, before adding the sugar. Once this has been added, you'll not want to boil for much longer than 20 minutes to reach setting point (see page 19), otherwise the fluid darkens and begins to taste more of caramel than of medlar. Ladle into small pots (heated in a low oven) whose entire contents can be used at one meal, and screw the lids on tightly. Store in a cool, dark place.

PAGES 72–73 *A medlar, from flower to fruit*

SOFT FRUIT

Rhubarb
Gooseberry
Raspberry
Blackcurrant
Redcurrant
Blackberry

Rhubarb

*G*enerally classified as fruit because of lending itself to fruit-like uses, rhubarb is as long-lived and hardy a plant as can be grown. In Orkney and the north of Scotland, it is encountered as the sole survivor of abandoned and ruined crofts, whose roofs were removed to avoid taxation. The culinary plant is a hybrid of several species, hailing from Siberia. At first used only medicinally – following its introduction in the sixteenth century – rhubarb took off as a culinary pleasure in the early years of the nineteenth century, when many named varieties were bred. It forces well and commercial forcing houses have been concentrated in Yorkshire. For garden use, there are special rhubarb forcing pots. I see little point in them myself. In my Sussex garden, I can pull rhubarb from about the last ten days of March, without any forcing. That is early enough for me.

Our rhubarb patch, at the furthest end of the vegetable garden, must have been planted when the Lloyds first came to Dixter, around 1911; and it is still in excellent health. There are two varieties (of whose naming I have no idea), one of them coming in a couple of weeks earlier than the other.

With rhubarb plants being so long-lived, there is always the danger of perennial weeds like couch grass or bindweed taking over. We manage to keep these more or less under control and our only other cultural duty is to apply a surface mulch of compost every winter.

Rhubarb is pulled, rather than picked. But I take a knife with me to the bed and immediately trim a sliver off the base of the stem, and trim off the leaf blade at the top. You can be sure that the entire stem will be tender during the first six weeks of the season, so there'll be no question of needing to peel off 'string'. By midsummer most of the foliage will have died, but rain in July will often start growth off again, and you can enjoy some late young stems.

The big white inflorescences of rhubarb are very handsome, in May. Gardeners habitually and traditionally remove them as soon as observed, their theory doubtless being that they weaken the plant. This can scarcely be noticeable, however, and I believe that the true reason is that it's a job that's easily accomplished and that produces obvious results with the minimum of effort. My standing order is that the flowering stems should not be removed. One

PAGE 74 *The blackcurrant 'Boskoop Giant'*
PAGE 75 *A summer-fruiting raspberry*

LEFT TO RIGHT *Growing rhubarb, flowering rhubarb stems, and rhubarb seedheads*

year there were none and I became irate. But it transpired that the plants had all decided not to flower that season. If picked before the pollen starts to shed, the inflorescence (given adequate support) looks well in large flower arrangements. A little later, the seedheads can be gathered for dried arrangements.

IN THE KITCHEN

The memory of being forced to eat rhubarb and glutinous custard when young because – like spinach – it was good for you, together with its later, similar appearance at school meals, has put many adults off it for life, which is a shame. However, I find that most of my young adult friends enjoy rhubarb as much as I do, so maybe the practice of forced feeding has ceased. There

78

are occasional gleams of progress to be discerned, in our civilization.

When eating rhubarb, I have a preference for seeing it in pleasantly coloured chunks, rather than disintegrated into an amorphous mass. Boiling results in the latter condition; baking, in the former. So, place your chopped-up stems, with sugar to taste (brown is nice), in a casserole or other covered dish. Cover, to prevent exposed bits from drying and hardening, but no water needs adding. Bake at 140°C/275°F/gas mark 1 for 50 minutes. The rhubarb pieces will keep their shape perfectly and will be swimming in their own juice. If you like stewed fruit at breakfast, rhubarb makes for variety.

My rhubarb recipes were mostly sent me by well-wishing pen friends, after they had read in *The Year at Great Dixter* that I had found little help in Jane Grigson on this fruit, since her dislike of it was inveterate. The first that I give came to me without a name; but is the one that I turn to most frequently. Perhaps I shall call it:

COMPÔTE OF RHUBARB WITH BANANA AND RUM

This quantity serves 4.

1lb rhubarb,
cut into 1½in pieces
Generous ½ cup sugar
Juice of 1 orange
Pinch of salt
2 bananas
1 tablespoon rum

Put the rhubarb into a bowl, sprinkle over the sugar, add the orange juice and then the salt. Leave overnight.

Bake in a preheated oven at 140°C/275°F/gas mark 1 in a covered container for 45 minutes. Cool. Dice the bananas and fold them in, together with the rum, turning the ingredients gently, so as to avoid breaking up the fragile rhubarb chunks. Serve chilled.

RHUBARB TART

This tart is well partnered by a good Sauternes, comments my godson Michael Schuster, from whom I had the recipe. Serves 8.

Sweet piecrust dough
1½ cups all-purpose flour
Generous ¼ cup superfine sugar
1 stick chilled butter, diced
Cold water to mix

Fruit filling
Generous 1 cup granulated sugar
Generous ¾ cup water
2lb rhubarb, chopped into 1in pieces

Lemon cream filling
4 egg yolks
Generous ½ cup superfine sugar
⅔ cup heavy cream
Finely grated peel of 1 lemon

To make the dough, sift together the flour and sugar, then cut in the butter. Work in just enough cold water to bind. Roll out to line a 10in tart pan. Leave it to rest in the refrigerator for 30 minutes.

Place a baking sheet in the oven and preheat to 190°C/375°F/gas mark 5. Pre-bake the dough for 15 minutes or so, until lightly coloured. Leave to cool.

To make the fruit filling, stir the sugar and water together over a medium heat till the sugar dissolves, then bring to a light boil. Add the rhubarb and simmer for one minute. Drain and reserve the rhubarb.

To make the lemon cream filling, beat the egg yolks and superfine sugar in a bowl with an electric beater for about 3 minutes, until the volume has tripled. Fold in the heavy cream and lemon peel.

Spread the rhubarb on the bottom of the tart, cover with cream filling and bake at 190°C/375°F/gas mark 5 for 25–30 minutes, until the cream filling is lightly browned. Sprinkle with extra sugar, if desired, and remove it from the pan on to a large plate. Leave to cool for about an hour before serving.

RHUBARB AND GINGER STEAMED SPONGE PUDDING

This quantity serves 4.

3 tablespoons syrup from
preserved stem ginger
8oz rhubarb,
cut into 1½in pieces
1 stick butter, softened
Generous ½ cup demerara sugar
Grated peel of 1 orange
2 eggs, separated
2 cups fresh breadcrumbs
1 teaspoon ground ginger
2 tablespoons preserved ginger, chopped
Little milk (if needed)

Butter a 5-cup (or, for comfort, 6-cup) deep, heatproof bowl. Put the ginger syrup in the bottom, then add the rhubarb.

Cream the butter with the demerara sugar and grated orange peel. Beat in the egg yolks. Fold in the breadcrumbs and ground ginger. Fold in the preserved ginger, adding a little milk if the mixture is too stiff. Beat the egg whites until stiff, then fold in. Transfer to the bowl, cover with a double layer of foil and steam for 2 hours (see pages 19–20). Turn out and serve with custard or cream.

RHUBARB AND DATE BAKE

Double quantity piecrust dough
(see page 12)
2lb rhubarb, cut into small pieces
Scant 1 cup chopped dates
Grated peel of 1 lemon
Ground cinnamon

Roll out half the dough and use it to line a shallow 10in tart pan. Leave to rest in the refrigerator for 30 minutes. Spread with a generous layer of the rhubarb mixed with chopped dates. Add the grated lemon peel and a sprinkling of cinnamon. Cover with the rest of the dough, rolled out more thinly. Press down well and lightly score the top, criss-cross fashion. Bake in a preheated oven at 190°C/375°F/gas mark 5 for 30 minutes or until well browned.

RHUBARB AND BANANA PIE

1lb rhubarb, chopped into 1in pieces
Grated peel of ½ lemon
Scant ½ cup granulated sugar
4 bananas
2 tablespoons superfine sugar
2 egg whites, stiffly beaten
½ cup slivered almonds

Place the rhubarb in a pie plate and sprinkle with the lemon peel and the granulated sugar. Peel, crush and beat to a pulp the bananas with the superfine sugar. Fold the stiffly beaten egg whites into the banana pulp, then spread the mixture on top of the rhubarb to form a crust. Sprinkle the top with the slivered almonds and bake in a preheated oven at 180°C/350°F/gas mark 4 for 30 minutes. Serve hot with cream.

Gooseberry

This is one of the few fruits that we deliberately eat unripe. The smaller the fruit, the more tender its skin but also the higher its acidity. The gooseberry is best grown on a long stem or leg, so that there is space between its lowest branches and the mulch beneath, although, inevitably, the weight of fruit will bring some down to the ground. Fruit is borne both along the young wood of the previous season, as in blackcurrants, and on spurs of older wood, as in redcurrants.

Pruning consists mainly in keeping the bush open, so that air can circulate freely within it. Cut out old branches in winter. Shorten back vigorous young ones by about half. Don't overfeed with nitrogen. Cuttings are rooted in the same way as redcurrants (see page 94), but normally one buys second-year bushes. The large-fruited dessert variety 'Leveller' is to be highly recommended, as it is just as good for culinary purposes and you can pick selectively with the aim of thinning the fruit. What remains can then be allowed to ripen. I am not all that enamoured of ripe gooseberries – just one now and again. Usually I leave them to the wasps.

The main pest both of gooseberries and of redcurrants (which are closely related), is the caterpillars of the gooseberry sawfly. If uncontrolled, these can defoliate entire bushes, hopelessly weakening them. The eggs are laid, sometimes as many as thirty to a leaf, on the undersides of the young foliage and you should spray against this pest very soon after blossom time, while the larvae are still small. Further generations may occur, later in the season, so watch out. And then there is mildew, which becomes apparent soon after flowering and often entirely cripples the bush, destroying foliage and crop. Luckily it is easily prevented, if you spray with a protective fungicide immediately after flowering. This should be done as a matter of course, whether you have spotted signs of the disease or not. One spraying seems to do the trick.

IN THE KITCHEN

Gooseberries are useful frozen. Pick them while still unripe (I do this in early June), while their skins are tender and the fruits barely half-grown. No need to sugar or blanch them. Just top and tail the fruits, wash them and freeze in boxes or bags.

GOOSEBERRY FOOL

This is the way I most often use gooseberries, being quick and simple to do and always popular with my friends. Serve with shortbread or some other sweet cookie.

4 tablespoons butter
1lb gooseberries, topped and tailed
Sugar
1¼ cups heavy or whipping cream

Melt the butter in a saucepan and add the gooseberries. If frozen, warm them very gently. When they are cooked and soft, remove from the heat and mash well with the back of a large wooden fork. Add sugar to taste, the amount depending on the ripeness of the fruit. Cool.

Whip the cream until floppy stiff. Turn in the fruit, gently. Chill before serving.

STEAMED GOOSEBERRY PUDDING

I remember the pleased surprise of some French guests to whom a Scottish friend, Alan Roger, gave this pudding, when they were visiting him in Wester Ross. Gooseberries scarcely come into the culinary repertoire of France. (With foreign guests, always serve food typical of your own country, rather than of theirs.

Admittedly it will, in the long term, be difficult to steer off the French cuisine.)

This is made with a suet crust pastry as given for *Steamed Mulberry Suet Pudding* (page 34), the cavity being filled with gooseberries, topped and tailed, brown sugar to taste and 2–4 tablespoons of butter. Steam for 3–4 hours (see pages 19–20).

GOOSEBERRY TART

A recipe given me by my Scottish friend Colin Hamilton.

1lb gooseberries, topped and tailed

Sweet pastry dough
1¾ cups all-purpose flour
1 tablespoon sugar
Pinch of salt
7 tablespoons butter, softened and diced
1 egg yolk
1 tablespoon heavy cream

Cream filling
⅔ cup heavy cream
2–3 egg yolks

1 teaspoon all-purpose flour
Scant ½ cup vanilla-flavoured sugar

Sift the flour, sugar and salt together into a mixing bowl. Make a well in the centre and put in the butter, egg yolk and cream. With the tips of your fingers, pinch the butter, egg and cream together. Use a metal spatula to cut the flour into the butter mixture, blending until the dough is crumbly. Add a teaspoon of water, or more, to make the dough cling together. Put it in a plastic bag and rest in the refrigerator or a cool place for 30 minutes.

Place a baking sheet in the oven and

Gooseberries ready for picking – in fact, more than ready; I try to pick them half-grown

preheat to 200°C/400°F/gas mark 6. Roll out the dough and use it to line a 10in tart pan (see page 21). On this place a closely packed single layer of gooseberries.

Put the ingredients for the cream filling in a bowl and whisk to combine. If there doesn't seem to be enough of the mixture, add a little more cream and milk mixed. Pour the filling over the gooseberries.

Remove from the tart pan while still warm. Serve cool sprinkled with sugar.

Raspberry

I do not grow strawberries, visiting the local 'Pick Your Own', which offers them over a long season. Raspberries are different. Not so exciting at the start of the season, maybe (though year-round strawberries, often of indifferent flavour, have cancelled out that particular thrill), but unbeatable for sustained guzzling. As with globe artichokes, I can eat fresh raspberries daily without becoming sated – certainly not the case with strawberries.

The development of autumn-fruiting raspberries has made a great difference to our lives. There was the 'Hailsham' berry, when I was a child, but that was never a great success. Modern varieties are at least as well flavoured as the traditional summer-fruiters. And, whereas summer raspberries have a limited season of some three weeks, the autumn-fruiters extend theirs over two months.

Another point: summer raspberries always, under garden conditions, need protecting against birds. By the time the autumn-fruiters come along, the birds have frequently (but not always) lost interest and they can be grown anywhere.

If you have a cage for your raspberries, as we do, there is the one great disadvantage, assuming you want to grow several varieties, of their intermingling, since all raspberries have a suckering habit. I made the mistake of planting a row of summer-fruiting 'Malling Delight' next to a row of autumn-fruiters. The latter were infiltrated by the former, which made nonsense of their pruning.

The June–July raspberries, such as 'Delight', crop only on the canes which they made in the previous year. So, after fruiting, you cut to the ground all their fruited canes and leave untouched those that are young and which will bear next year's fruit. In the course of the winter, the weakest of these new canes will be removed, but the rest will merely be shortened at the tips.

The autumn-fruiting raspberries crop on their young canes of the current season's making. Their pruning, in winter, is to cut to the ground everything in sight. If 'Delight' has infiltrated, you are also cutting down its provision for next year's fruiting. So, grow your summer- and autumn-fruiters separately and, for preference, separate every variety from every other, so that there can be no kind of mix-up, with stronger varieties overwhelming the weaker.

Raspberries enjoy rich living. We renew a heavy mulch of garden compost every year. And in early spring we always apply a general fertilizer containing

Raspberry canes – not yet tipped – in the fruit cage

nitrogen, phosphate and potash, at 3–4oz per square yard. That acts as a boost to growth and helps to rot the compost down. The compost also has the useful effect of retaining soil moisture. We can never spare the time or water to irrigate the fruit cage, so moisture retention is of great importance when a summer drought develops, which it nearly always does. My local 'Pick Your Own', which is without irrigation, got virtually no crop from their 'Autumn Bliss' raspberries in 1995, thanks to drought. It's something of a can't win situation, because a wet summer ruins the fruit, which goes down to botrytis, the grey mould fungus. And flavour is anyway much impaired.

My main summer-fruiter, 'Malling Delight', has extremely large, mushy fruits, which are served ideally by a dry spell. It is too wet a fruit to freeze satisfactorily. Then I have a few plants of 'Leo', which also fruits on its old canes, but rather later, running into August.

After that, we come to the autumn crop on young canes and I have grown 'Zeva' (a Swiss variety), 'Heritage' (American) and 'Fallgold' (American). 'Zeva' has a wonderful flavour but is a poor cropper and none too vigorous. 'Heritage' is small-fruited, bright red, but has been swamped by its neighbours. 'Fallgold' is vigorous and invades its weaker brethren. Its yellow fruits are exceptionally sweet, though weak on flavour. In a drought season, honey bees go for it (as for peaches), in search of something sweet and moist.

'Autumn Bliss' (bred by Elizabeth Bliss at East Malling Research Station in Kent) is far superior to any of the above. Indeed, I consider its flavour richer than that of my summer-fruiters. It grows in a patch of its own, away from the cage.

Raspberry-picking is a ploy for which it is always easy to find willing guests, thinking of cream and of the next meal. They will unfailingly pick too many, whatever the size of the bowl provided, heaping the berries up into a kind of ant hill, so that they are rolling off the edge.

IN THE KITCHEN

Having been in fresh raspberries more or less continuously for four months, I do not mind giving them a rest for the other eight, so I don't keep them in the freezer. But they do have a reputation for performing well in the freezer. Frozen individually in a single layer on small trays before being packed into freezer bags, the berries will emerge in winter in good condition.

In my culinary use of raspberries, I am unadventurous. Provided there is

sugar and cream, I am happy. I don't have a high opinion of raspberry jam. If you are making it, do include some redcurrant juice. It adds a welcome sharpness and it helps the jam to set. Simmer the raspberries very gently in their own juice for about 20 minutes, until they are soft. Add sugar: 1¾ cups of sugar to 1lb of fruit. Cook the currants separately, just long enough to draw their juice, pass them through a strainer and add to the raspberry and sugar mixture. (For general directions on jam-making, see pages 18–19.)

Raspberry 'Autumn Bliss'

SUMMER PUDDING

A pudding that I make once a year, following Jane Grigson's advice to serve with 'a great deal of cream'. As she wrote, 'cream is essential for this strong-flavoured pudding, which because of its flavour goes a long way and should be served in small slices.'

2lb raspberries and redcurrants,
roughly in proportion 4:1
1½ cups sugar
about 10 slices good white bread,
one day old, with crusts removed

Place the fruit and sugar in a bowl and leave overnight. Next day tip them into a pan, stir gently, bring to a boil and simmer for 2–3 minutes or until there is plenty of juice. Taste, add more sugar if necessary, and set aside.

Line a 5-cup deep bowl with the bread cut into ¼–½in wide slices. Make a circle for the bottom of the bowl and line the sides so that there are no gaps. Spoon in half the fruit, cover with a layer of bread, pour in the remainder of the fruit and the juice. Cover with another layer of bread and trim to make a neat finish. Place a plate or saucer on top, weight it and leave the pudding overnight – or for several days in the refrigerator.

Run a thin knife between the pudding and the bowl, place a serving plate upside down on top, and turn out quickly, just before needed. Serve accompanied with cream, and extra sugar if required.

RASPBERRY AND REDCURRANT TART

A recipe given me by Colin Hamilton. Marvellous to follow a rich main course, like turbot or brill served with a cream or fish sauce. It's made with a sweet pastry which is very like Jane Grigson's creamed *pâte sucrée* (see page 21).

1½lb raspberries
½lb redcurrants

Generous ¾ cup sugar
1 tablespoon redcurrant jelly (see page 96), to glaze

Sweet pastry dough
1 stick butter, softened
3 tablespoons sugar
1 egg
Pinch of salt
1½ cups all-purpose flour

To make the pastry dough, cream the butter and sugar, add the egg and salt and mix in the flour, working the dough as little as possible. Put it in a plastic bag and rest in the refrigerator or a cool place for 30 minutes.

Roll out the dough to fit a 10in tart pan (see page 21). Leave to rest again, for 30 minutes to an hour. Place a baking sheet in the oven and preheat to 180°C/350°F/gas mark 4. Pre-bake the tart shell for 20 minutes. Allow to cool.

Put the fruit and sugar in a pan and cook for a few minutes only. The fruit should keep its shape but a lot of juice should run out. Transfer the strained fruit to the cooled tart shell and return to the oven, at 180°C/350°F/gas mark 4, for 10 minutes.

Meanwhile, add the redcurrant jelly to the juice and reduce the mixture by boiling (but not for too long!). This will provide a thick glaze. Pour it over the fruit after the tart has cooled.

Raspberry 'Malling Delight'

Blackcurrant

The flavour of blackcurrants was too strong and personal for my liking as a child, but I grew out of that. I wish that all my friends would similarly grow up. Few Americans relish blackcurrants and the French only as a drink.

The smell of a blackcurrant plant is characteristically strong. When you find a currant seedling anywhere (birds freely distribute the seeds), pinch and smell a leaf. If it's a black one, the smell will leave you in no doubt.

While the habit of flowering and fruiting in redcurrants and gooseberries is similar, that of the blackcurrant is entirely different, as has to be its pruning. Instead of a permanent framework, you have a bush that is totally renewed over a period of three years or so. This is because it crops along the length of young wood made in the previous summer. Your object is to promote the production of abundant young wood. To this end, you remove branches that have cropped and that are putting on decreasingly strong young shoots. After three years, you can remove the entire branch, with a saw, at ground level. The strongest young wood on a blackcurrant is sent up from near to or even below ground level. Young shoots for fruiting are never shortened, always left full length. The pruning of blackcurrants is warming work, good for a frosty winter's day. I do everything of this kind from a kneeling mat, but have to move around the bush to get myself in the most convenient position.

As a general comment, it should be said that amateur gardeners tend to hold on to their currant bushes, of whatever kind, for far too long. If they have served you for eight or ten years, 'they don't owe you nothing', as Albert Croft, my very Sussex gardener, used to say. If possible, buy your plants from a specialist firm raising its own stock; some ropy old stuff finds its way on to the open market.

When choosing which variety to grow, remember that all the more modern kinds have been bred with a view to their commercial suitability. That may well not tally with what would suit you best. The commercial blackcurrant is apt to have a thick skin, enabling it to travel well without being damaged. In the garden, what we most want is a large, thin-skinned fruit of luscious juiciness and flavour. I think 'Boskoop Giant' (see page 74) unbeatable in meeting these desiderata.

The customer likes to see what he considers value for money, so the year-old plant you should buy will have a couple of young branches on it. Cut these hard back to the base, on planting. You should want to put strength into your plants and must sacrifice any thought of a crop in the first season.

Plant in well-manured ground at a spacing of at least 5ft. Blackcurrants are gross feeders, so incorporate plenty of well-rotted, bulky organic manure. From the time fruiting starts, I have a permanent mulch of composted grass from our meadows spread over the surface; not the best-rotted compost from the centre of the heap, but less decayed material from near the outside. One effect of this is to retain moisture in time of drought; another, to prevent mud from splashing the fruit. Currants and other soft fruit are also included in the application, at 4oz to the square yard, of the general fertilizer with which we visit all the borders in early spring.

I shan't go into pests and diseases, except to suggest that you apply a systemic aphicide, in early summer, when leaves have become distorted and bloated with red tumours.

If you are picking blackcurrants for a fool or for ice-cream, there'll be no need to worry about stalks. But if I want clean, stalk-free fruit and am picking it myself, I often find it least trouble, in the long run, to pick off the fruits, individually, from their stalks, as I go along, using both hands for the job. With large-fruited 'Boskoop Giant', this isn't the chore it may sound.

I N   T H E   K I T C H E N

I find it worthwhile to freeze blackcurrants as they have a relatively short season. It is a simple job to do: just pack them in plastic boxes or bags and put them in the deep-freeze. There is no need to strip them from their stalks (though we do) or to add sugar.

B L A C K C U R R A N T   F O O L

This can be made at any season from currants that have been deep-frozen.

Stew 1lb of unstrigged fruit, fresh or frozen, with a suitable quantity of sugar, according to the ripeness of the fruit, but remembering that cream itself has a sweetening influence. Pass through a fine strainer (blackcurrant pips are small). Add the cooled pulp and juice to 1¼ cups of whipped cream that is still on the floppy side. Turn in the juices gently with a large spoon, not losing too many air bubbles in the process. Transfer to a pretty bowl and chill. Serve with shortbread or some sweet cookie.

BLACKCURRANT ICE-CREAM

The advantage of such an ice-cream (and it can also be made with loganberries or tayberries) is the freshness of the uncooked fruit. This flavour is lost if the ice is kept for longer than a few weeks.

1lb blackcurrants, unstrigged
¾ cup sugar
½ cup water
1¼ cups heavy or whipping cream

Put the fruit in a blender and whiz for 5 seconds – just long enough to release the juices and to make the next operation less laborious. Now pound the pulp through a fine strainer.

Put the sugar and water into a saucepan set over medium heat and stir until the sugar dissolves. Then bring to a boil and boil for a couple of minutes. Stir the syrup into the pulp and turn, with a large spoon, into the cream which has been whipped not too stiff; just floppy.

Turn into a bowl, cover with plastic wrap and place in the deep-freeze. When starting to set, after about 3 hours, bring it out and beat vigorously until all lumps have been removed. Then back into the freezer for another 3 hours. Remove to a cool room temperature at about the time you are starting your meal. Turn out into a suitably coloured bowl and eat with shortbread cookies, or something equivalent.

BLACKCURRANT PUDDING

1lb blackcurrants, strigged
Generous ¾ cup sugar

Suet crust
2 cups self-rising flour
8oz suet, grated
Pinch of salt
Cold water to mix

Prepare and roll out the suet dough as for *Steamed Mulberry Suet Pudding* (see page 34). Save a quarter for the lid and use the rest to line a buttered 5-cup, deep, heatproof bowl.

Mix the blackcurrants with the sugar. Fill the bowl, not quite to the rim, with the sugared fruit. Apply the dough lid and follow the instructions for covering and steaming given on pages 19–20. Steam for at least 3 hours (longer if you like a crisp crust).

Serve with abundant cream. Yummy.

Redcurrant

*T*he only difference between red and white currants is in their colour. As the chief glory of the redcurrant is its colour, I see no point in growing the anaemic white, except to be different. There are more interesting ways of being different than this. Admittedly, white currants do take on a pink flush, when cooked with sugar, but nothing to boast about.

Both the overwintering flower and leaf buds of redcurrants, as well as their fruit, are popular with birds. In order to avoid developing high blood pressure and a great bird hate ('After I've fed them through the winter, this is all the reward I receive . . .'), it is wise to grow them in a bird-proof enclosure (unlike mine, which, although intended as a fruit cage, is sometimes more like a bird cage).

The bush is trained to form a permanent framework, eventually up to 1.8m/6ft high and with a somewhat open centre, so as to admit plenty of light. From the first, it is trained on a permanent, branch-free leg. If you buy your bush (one may be enough; two bushes at the most, unless you consume large quantities of redcurrant jelly), the leg will already be there. If you are striking your own cuttings, they should be of young, current season's wood, up to 1ft long and with the weaker, thinner top bit removed back to a strong bud. Rub out all the buds along this cutting, except the top three. Make a hole in the ground with a piece of cane so that when the cutting is dropped or pushed in, the bottom comes into contact with the bottom of the hole and 6in remains above ground. Firm in. It'll be the third year before the bush is cropping.

Build up a framework by shortening back each strong shoot to 6in long. Make your pruning cut just above a bud. Sometimes you'll find that there are two buds in the same position. Rub out one of them. Badly placed branches that will clutter up the centre of the bush, or that are too close to their neighbours, should be cut hard back to within ½in of the base.

The crop is borne from flower/fruit buds clustered at the base of young shoots, and also on spurs that will have developed along older wood. Routine pruning, each winter, consists of shortening the leaders, as described, and of spurring hard back any other growths. Feed the bushes as for blackcurrants (see page 92), but with less nitrogen. By keeping a mulch of straw or compost beneath them, you will ensure that the fruit remains clean.

Sawfly caterpillars are a major pest, as with gooseberries (see page 83).

The fruit is generally ripe in the second half of July and remains in decent condition on the bush for quite a while. But pectin content gradually decreases, so you should not defer the making of jelly too long.

Redcurrant jelly (surprisingly difficult to find for sale) is the only serious use that I have for this fruit. However, its colour and shine adds lustre to a fruit salad. I also include redcurrants in *Summer Pudding* (see page 89), made once a year, and I occasionally make *Raspberry and Redcurrant Tart* (see page 90).

R E D C U R R A N T   J E L L Y

Pick and wash the fruit and stew it in a preserving pan with only enough water to prevent initial burning. Simmer till all the juice has been released and then pass through a jelly bag. The juice is so free that, within minutes, only skin and stems will remain in the bag and there will be no temptation to squeeze it, a practice which anyway makes the sample cloudy.

Bring the juice to boiling point in your pan and at the same time warm the sugar – 2½ cups to each 2½ cups of juice – in the oven. Add the one to the other and boil hard (watch that it doesn't froth over the top) until setting point is reached – not more than 20 minutes. (See page 19 for testing setting point and potting.)

Once the sugar has been added, boiling will darken the sample, quite spoiling its appearance (and flavour) if continued for too long. If you have reason to believe that the juice is on the wet side, and none too concentrated, boil and reduce it for 10 minutes or so before adding the sugar.

C U M B E R L A N D   S A U C E

Another use for redcurrants is in Cumberland Sauce, which is based on redcurrant jelly, and is an excellent accompaniment for boiled ham. I give my mother's recipe, which she picked up in Germany, when visiting her friends in Frankfurt am Main. There, they pronounced it with a heavy German accent, making two syllables of 'sauce'.

Lena's recipe. Frankfurt a/M. Nov. 1928

Peel of 1 orange, grated, and
1 tablespoonful of juice
1 breakfast cupful of redcurrant jelly,
heated and passed through a strainer
[I use a 1lb pot of jelly]
1 teaspoonful of English mustard

Pinch of salt and pepper
1 dessertspoonful of red wine

Mix well together and eat with saddle of
mutton, goose, duck, venison, hare or ham.

Blackberry

I do not, voluntarily, grow brambles (as the fruit is known in Scotland and the north of England) in my garden, but they are in hedgerows and woods around me and blackberrying is one of my favourite autumn recreations – usually by myself. If a dog accompanies me, she gets bored and wonders why I don't get a move on. (Mushrooming is even more irritating, as there's no knowing which direction I shall take next and I'm never getting anywhere.)

I quite like commercially grown blackberries, even though their flavour is not outstanding. Ripe cultivated blackberries, eaten raw with cream and sugar, are a pleasant change from my usual breakfast of stewed apples.

I do not know anything about their botanical classification, but there are two quite distinct varieties of blackberry in my part of England (East Sussex). Around the margins of woodland, and above all in coppiced areas, grows a shiny-fruited kind with large drupels. It ripens from mid-August and has a tendency to sourness and lack of flavour, though acceptable enough if found in quantities that can be quickly picked.

The second kind, which monopolizes the hedgerows, does not ripen until the end of September. This has numerous small drupels and, when ripe, is very sweet and aromatic. It is the one I go for. Before mechanical hedge-trimming came in, it used to fruit in far larger quantities. On a good stand, I could pick nearly 4lb in an hour. But a bramble cane takes two years to mature, so there's little scope for heavy crops nowadays.

Still, out I go. There are hazards. You need to look out for wasps, for instance. When I was stationed in Suffolk, during the war, hornets were avid feeders on blackberries. We don't get them around us. Last time I went out, there were four of my neighbour's rams in the field (once an orchard) that we lease to him. One of them was lively. He took me unawares, at the first charge, and knocked my basket, and the few blackberries in it, out of my hand. I was ready for him after that. The best defence, I found, was to kick his hard nose on its ridge, as he advanced, head lowered. After a time, he tired and I resumed my picking. However, you cannot simultaneously look into a hedge and keep an eye on what's going on behind. I suddenly found myself sprawling in sheep's dung, having been charged plumb in the middle of my behind. Never having had any dignity to stand on, I found this hilarious, but there was no one else to enjoy the occasion, except in the retelling.

If you have it in mind to make bramble jelly (which is best of all), you need to gather a proportion of partially unripe, reddish fruit, as this will contain a reasonable amount of the pectin needed to set the jelly. You cannot pick with one hand at any speed. The fruit needs to be sufficiently prolific to warrant setting your basket (which must have a broad, flat bottom) on the ground, while you set to with both hands, alternately holding the truss steady with one hand, while picking with the other. If there's a ditch between you and the hedge, it makes life more difficult, but I don't think it worth bringing with you a crook-handled walking stick to pull the out-of-reach trusses towards you. It all takes too long.

B R A M B L E   J E L L Y

Use as many brambles as you can pick, as yield is always poor. There's no need to wash the fruit if you live in clean air (where lichens thrive on trees and shrubs). Picking by busy road verges, where exhaust fumes are constantly contaminating the fruit, is hardly to be recommended, even if you do wash it.

Pile the blackberries into a preserving pan and add not quite enough water to cover. (The more you add, the more will later have to be evaporated.) I also add 2 teaspoons of tartaric acid to help the set. Stew gently until the fruit is soft and all the juice has run out that will run out. Ladle the pulp and juice into a jelly bag (see page 70) suspended above a mixing bowl. Leave to drip overnight.

Next day it may be worth squeezing the bag for a bit more juice if there's someone with strong hands to keep it closed at the mouth while the squeezer gets to work. Measure the juice and return it to the pan. Heat to boiling point and then add sugar, warmed in a low oven, at the rate of 2½ cups to each 2½ cups of juice. Boil fast till setting point is reached (see page 19).

Use a small mug to ladle the juice into preheated jars and screw their lids on tightly forthwith. Store in a cool, dark place.

B L A C K B E R R Y   F O O L

Put 2½ cups fresh or frozen blackberries in a saucepan with a scant ½ cup of sugar and the juice of half a lemon and heat, slowly at first. After simmering for 10 minutes, push the pan contents through a strainer. Leave to cool. Whip 1¼ cups heavy or whipping cream till fairly thick; then gently fold in the fruit juice and pulp. Pour into a bowl and chill. Serve with shortbread.

If the berries yield a great deal more juice than pulp, you are in danger of finishing with soup rather than a reasonably stiff fool. You may not need to add all the juice to the whipped cream.

BLACKBERRY AND APPLE PIE

Softish 'Bramley's' are a good choice of apple for this pie, as they cook quickly.

You will find my method for piecrust dough on page 12, but the instructions for assembling the pie are given below.

1lb cooking apples, peeled and cored
1½ cups blackberries
Scant ½ cup sugar
1½ quantities piecrust dough

Into a medium-sized rimmed pie dish, slice the peeled and cored cooking apples. Sprinkle in the blackberries and sugar. The pie dish contents should be mounded a little above the rim.

Sprinkle flour on to a board and on to your rolling pin and roll out the dough to the shape of the dish but 1in larger. Cut out a 1in strip around the perimeter and, having first dampened the dish rim with water, fit the dough strip on to it, pressing it firmly. Dampen that and next fit the rest of the dough over it to form a lid. Knock up the edges with the side of your thumb.

By the time you have trimmed around the edge of the pie dish with a vertically held knife, there'll be a little dough left over. I am no artist but there'll always, in my experience, be someone handy to shape the dough that remains into a decoration, which is then applied to the top of the pie. One friend depicted my two dachshunds among clumps of rushes. It is surprising what talents the opportunity brings out.

Place a baking sheet in the oven and preheat to 180°/350°F/gas mark 4. Brush the dough with milk and sprinkle on a dusting of sugar. Make a blow-hole slit in the top of the pie with the tip of a knife. Bake for 40 minutes.

Serve hot with pouring cream. Having first exhibited the baked pie all around the table, for its decoration, now appetizingly bronzed, to be admired, it is usually least messy to cut up and serve the pie yourself, rather than pass it around.

ROOT VEGETABLES

Carrot
Beet
Potato
Jerusalem Artichoke

Parsnip
Celeriac
Leek
Shallot & Garlic

Carrot

We take for granted the bright orange colouring of carrots, but this has been obtained and retained by selection. In the United States and in France, it is possible to buy seed of white or off-white carrots, which is the colour of the root of the wild plant, but I see no conceivable point in foregoing the wonderful carrot orange, which enlivens so many dishes in the same way as do beet and tomato.

Carrot, *Daucus carota*, is found wild in most of Europe, including Britain, and is widespread, in a feral state, in the United States. It is the plant referred to there as Queen Anne's Lace, whereas we generally apply that name to cow parsley, *Anthriscus sylvestris* (though also, loosely, to almost any wild white-flowered umbellifer below the size of hogweed).

In the markets, this is a year-round crop, but the forced roots of early spring taste of nothing. Young carrots, grown without forcing, have a specially delicious flavour which is lost as they mature, but the different taste of mature carrots, fresh from the ground, has its own excellence. It is an incredibly sweet vegetable (as is the related parsnip) and can be used for cakes, puddings and jams, as well as for more usual savoury purposes.

The greatest bind, in growing carrots, is its parasite, the carrot root fly. The maggots of this insect feed on carrot roots (as also, generally to a less serious degree, on parsley, celery, celery root and parsnip) and make a horrible, black, pulpy mess where they have been. They can continue to feed on stored roots.

There are two generations of this fly, the second being only partial. Your worst trials will be from spring sowings. We therefore delay all ours, making them between mid-June and early July. There is now an effective commercially produced fleece that prevents the fly from approaching your carrots. After they have been thinned, you insert strong wire hoops over the carrot rows, spread the fleece over them and fix it into the ground on each side with stout lengths of wire bent at the top end to make a crook, effectively like a hairpin.

Carrots should not be grown in ground that has been freshly manured. The seeds being small, the tilth must be fine. Sow ½in deep in rows 12in apart. You must hope there won't be heavy rain after this, especially on heavy ground like

PAGE 100 *Shallots almost ready for harvest*
PAGE 101 *Beets, just pulled*

ours, as this will pan and subsequently harden and crack, making it difficult for the seedlings to penetrate the crust. Seedlings are thinned to 4in apart.

Types of carrot are classified as stump-rooted, intermediate and long. Long carrots look good, when well grown, on the show bench. As the best soil, especially over clay, is near to the surface, I make use of this fact by always growing the stump-rooted 'Early Nantes'. It is just as effective for late crops as for early and is a convenient size and shape, not more than 6in long, for handling in the kitchen. It never, until sprouting in the spring, develops a woody core that needs to be cut out.

IN THE KITCHEN

Besides topping and tailing them, carrots are nearly always the better for being scraped with the edge of a knife. Wet the root first and scrape the shine off the surface. Whenever carrots are to be boiled, reduce loss of flavour into the water by cooking them whole, or as near to whole as is practicable (another reason for growing shorter-rooted kinds). You can cut them after cooking. Of course, if all the liquid will eventually be used, as in soups, or absorbed, as when glazing, nothing will be lost by slicing the carrots at the start.

CRECY SOUP

I prefer this Grigson recipe from *Good Things* to the variant in her *Vegetable Book*. I always have homemade chicken stock in the freezer (see page 13). This quantity serves 3.

1½ cups sliced carrots
1 onion, chopped
8 tablespoons butter
2 tablespoons rice
3¾ cups light stock, heated
Sprig of thyme
Slices of white bread,
crusts removed and diced

Simmer the carrots and onion in a covered pan with 4 tablespoons of the butter for about 10 minutes. Don't let them brown. Add the rice, the hot stock and the sprig of thyme. Cook gently for 20 to 30 minutes. Remove the thyme and liquidize the soup, adding more stock if necessary. Reheat. Stir in 2 tablespoons of butter just before serving. Meanwhile, fry the bread dice in the last 2 tablespoons of butter.

GLAZED CARROTS VICHY STYLE

This is adapted from *Jane Grigson's Vegetable Book*.

Slice 6 carrots diagonally. Put them into a covered pan with a little water so that they are as much steaming as boiling. Add 1 tablespoon of butter and 1 teaspoon of sugar, with just a pinch of salt. Cook till the carrots are tender and the liquid reduced to a small amount of shiny, colourless glaze. These two moments should coincide (!!), which means you must watch to see that the glaze does not caramelize. Correct the seasoning and serve sprinkled with parsley.

Old carrots can be boiled whole for 5 minutes, before proceeding as above.

CARROT AND CELERIAC AU GRATIN

Good as a light meal on its own (serves 4) but also accompanies white fish or gammon well.

6 fair-sized, mature carrots
1 celeriac root
Chicken stock (see page 13)

Sauce
2 tablespoons butter
2 tablespoons all-purpose flour
1 tablespoon *each* grated Gruyère and
Parmesan cheese, mixed together

Top, tail and scrape the carrots. Cut each into four lengthways, then dice. Peel the celeriac root and cut into larger dice than the carrot. Put all into a pan with not quite enough cold water to cover, but top up with chicken stock. Bring to the boil and simmer gently for 15 to 20 minutes, until tender.

Drain, reserving the stock, and tip the vegetables into a gratin dish to keep warm, if the meal is immediately to follow. However, all but the final reheating can be done in advance.

Make a thinnish sauce with the butter and flour and the reserved stock. Remove from the heat and stir in the cheese. Pour evenly over the vegetables and scatter a little more grated Parmesan over the top. Cook in a hot oven (220°C/425°F/gas mark 7) till browning on top. This would take 10 minutes if already warm or 20 minutes if from cold. You might need the help of the broiler at the end.

Beet

What is it about beet that puts many people off one of the sweetest, most colourful and individual of vegetables? Individuality is, as we know of people, one of the most disputable of virtues, one man's meat being another's poison. The colour itself, which seems to me to bring a joyful variety into dishes (say, of white fish, potato and cauliflower or even leek), which would otherwise remain anaemic, may strike some as over the top and so vigorously staining as to endanger every contesting neighbour.

What about flavour? Here, I believe, is the crux. At school and in other circumstances where we have been subjected to institutional food, beets pickled in malt vinegar have all too frequently been the disgusting accompaniment to cold meat. It doesn't taste of beet at all, just of the aggressive vinegar, but the experience is enough to put many off the innocent partner for life. I never try to disguise beet's natural flavour, and friends who had thought they could not cope with it have discovered, and welcomed, its true nature.

Jane Grigson was not a convert. She had to go through the motions of being fair, in her *Vegetable Book*, but her introduction to the subject makes her feelings clear. 'We do not seem to have had much success with beetroot in this country. Perhaps this is partly the beetroot's fault. It is not an inspiring vegetable.' She does later concede that 'beetroot has a subtle flavour when not soused in malt vinegar.'

It is an easy crop to grow, provided the site is open and receives maximum light. The ground should have been dug and manured in the previous winter or autumn. There is no point in sowing early; the resulting seedlings are all too likely to bolt, if the weather turns cold. Mid-spring (with us, early May) is soon enough. A couple of later sowings, up to July, are a good idea because, although beet will hold in maturity for months, it is never quite so delicious as when only half-grown. In extreme old age, it becomes irredeemably tough.

I grow two kinds, one that is globe-shaped and another (twice as much of this) that is long and cylindrical. The latter would be awkward for boiling, being too long to fit into a saucepan, but once I had discovered that beet cooks best when baked in foil, this problem disappeared and the long root, of equal diameter for most of its length, actually becomes an advantage in the handling.

It is possible to buy seed of a dirty yellowish-fleshed beet, called 'Burpee's

Golden' – a disgusting colour, I thought, when I once made the mistake of growing it. 'The foliage can also be used in exactly the same way as spinach,' we are told, and this is true. But true also of any beet. You can go on using the young leaves long after the roots that you never got around to eating have become too tough. You should gather the leaf blades yourself, leaving the stems behind (which means that no preparation is necessary in the kitchen), drain them well after boiling, squeezing out the moisture, and finish off with plentiful butter and seasoning. Following a mild winter, beets will survive till spring, growth will be resumed, and regular, frequent pickings can be made of foliage and young shoots. The beet's main object at this stage being to run up to flower, you can foil its attempts. And this, remember, at a season when few fresh greens are around. I first met this excellent treatment in an American friend's kitchen (Wayne Winterrowd's). I can't imagine why we neglect it in Britain. No cook book that I've come across gives it a thought.

Overwintered beet shoots

Beet's season of use, fresh from the open ground, lasts from midsummer to the end of the year. Beets can be stored, in a cool, reasonably frost-free place, best in moist (not wet) sand. In the shops, it is quite difficult to find beets that have not already been cooked, which means that its usage has already been largely decided.

The knobbly 'seed' is actually a cluster of seeds, so your sowing should be sparse and thinning of the seedlings will be obligatory, eventually to 9in apart. There are now a few 'mono' seed strains, which produce seedlings singly. Pulling of beet for the kitchen is always easy, no digging involved, as most of the root stands above ground level.

Always handle gently, as a beet is all too prone to bleeding its goodness away, if damaged. Twist the leaves off; don't cut them. And never cut the root up before cooking it.

A globe-shaped beet almost ready to pull

IN THE KITCHEN

Scrubbing beet should be more a question of stroking the mud off. Leave the rat's-tail tap root intact. Bending it won't hurt. To cook the beets, I wrap the roots very loosely in a doubled sheet of foil, lay them on a baking sheet and bake slowly, at 150°C/300°F/gas mark 2 for three hours, normally. (One and a half to two hours will be long enough for young beets, four hours may be needed for old.) The foil being loose will prevent pressure points on the beet that would harden the skin and make peeling it difficult. Alternatively, round beets can be boiled, but for not more than two hours, or as little as 40 minutes for small, young beets.

When cooked, the skin should just slip off; you can do this bare-handed if

Pulling, at the same time thinning, beets

the beet is held under running cold water. I then lay the beets, seasoned, in a serving dish, chopping them up as little as possible, as this simply dissipates the heat. A lot of people are unused to eating hot beets, but I think it the nicest way. It goes excellently with white fish of all kinds, with hot ox-tongue (and that's so good) and with boiled, smoked ham on the bone.

BEETS BAKED WITH CREAM AND PARMESAN CHEESE

Up to 20 small young round beets
Salt and pepper
About 2 tablespoons chopped chives
1¼ cups light cream
½ cup grated Parmesan cheese
Few flecks of butter

Bake or boil the beets (see page 108). Slip them out of their skins and lay them in a buttered gratin dish. Season and sprinkle with the chopped chives, and add the cream, the grated Parmesan and some flecks of butter.

Bake in a preheated oven at 200°C/400°F/gas mark 6 till spotted golden brown.

BEET SALAD WITH ANCHOVIES

Serves 4 to 6 as an appetizer, but makes a good light main course for 2 (followed by cheese). When hard-boiling eggs, 8 minutes is about right. Much longer than that, the yolk loses its freshness.

1½lb young beets, cooked
2 eggs
1 2oz can anchovy fillets
1 shallot *or* 4 scallions
1½ slices bread (preferably whole-wheat), made into crumbs
1–2 tablespoons olive oil
Vinaigrette dressing (see page 183)
1–2 sprigs fresh dill, chopped
Flat-leaved parsley, chopped

Bake the beets in foil for not more than 2 hours, or if preferred, boil for 40 minutes or so (see page 108). Meanwhile, hard-boil and chop the eggs. Cut the anchovy fillets into snippets, and chop the shallot or scallions very finely. Turn the breadcrumbs in the olive oil and cook in a dry skillet, stirring, until pale gold and crisp.

Cool the cooked beets under a cold tap, slip off the skins and slice thinly. Lay on a flattish dish and dress with vinaigrette dressing.

Mix the eggs, shallot and herbs. Scatter over the beets and sprinkle the anchovies and breadcrumbs on top. Serve cold.

Potato

Virtually the only potatoes I grow are the salad kinds, which are waxy. These can be difficult to buy here, as the British prefer a floury potato. For baking, roasting, boiling and mashing, I depend on other growers. There are better uses for the space in my garden.

By far my favourite salad potato is the old English maincrop variety 'Pink Fir Apple', lifted in early autumn or when the haulm (stems and foliage) has died off. It has a pink skin and is extraordinarily shaped – long and thin, with frequent knobs and branches – but by no means impossible to handle. In America, 'Rose Thin Apple' is said to be similar, if not identical. The rather similar 'Ratte' is a variety that suppliers will try to push on you in lieu of 'Pink Fir Apple'. I presume that it is easier for them to multiply. But its flavour is less good and it does not keep through the winter. By February, ours will be sprouting incontinently, even under good storage conditions, while 'Pink Fir Apple' holds on. You should place your order for seed potatoes early. We normally get ours in by the end of October, but preferably a month before that, so as not to be disappointed. The suppliers are generally kind enough not to deliver before March. A fairly waxy, second early variety that has given me satisfaction is 'Charlotte'. It makes quite a large, smooth tuber.

I generally buy 'seed' (not literally seed, but smallish tubers) for chitting or sprouting, every third year, which is when my own saved stock (and probably yours also) often becomes virus-infected and greatly weakened in performance. There is really nothing to be done about this.

CULTIVATING POTATOES

The ground for potatoes needs to be well dug with manure or garden compost incorporated in plenty, and it should be rather loose at planting. If we leave planting until mid- or even late April we generally avoid damage by frost to the young shoots. If they are frosted, new growth will come, but the growing season will have been shortened somewhat. Before planting, the tubers should be chitted – that is, laid out in a single layer on trays in a cool, frost-free, light spot, so that the shoot buds can begin to sprout. These should be

A 'Pink Fir Apple' root, newly lifted

110

purple and quite stubby, like large crumbs, at planting.

The tubers are set into 5in-deep trenches, some 15–18in apart, with 24in between rows. The soil is then drawn back to level, or to leave a slight ridge over the potatoes. As these grow, soil is drawn up from between the rows so as to support the developing shoots. In practice, at Dixter, we do it only once, at that moment when the haulm is so tall as to be in danger of collapse if not supported. As well as supporting the shoots, earthing up encourages tuber formation at the base of the stems and prevents these tubers from seeing light and hence turning green. It also gives the opportunity of loosening the soil, so that water can penetrate, and of weeding.

Weeds are no problem once the potato haulm has covered the plot, but the weight of the crop materially depends on how much water reaches the plot at the time when growth is at its most vigorous. Irrigation will make a vast difference here. You only have to look at the monster irrigation appliances on commercial crops, seldom out of action even when it's raining, to appreciate this. Water is expensive and it is not being applied for fun.

Winter storage presents its own risks. The main hazard is that your potatoes will be got at by mice or rats without your noticing. Again, the tubers must be frost-free, yet cold, so as not to shrivel; and they must be kept dark, otherwise they turn green and are unpleasant, even indigestible, to eat.

CONTROLLING POTATO BLIGHT

However, the greatest bind in potato growing is potato blight, the disease which led to famine in Ireland in the middle of the nineteenth century, and which is caused by the fungus *Phytophthora infestans*. Starting as brown patches on the foliage, it spreads alarmingly fast, especially in damp or wet weather, exuding a most unpleasantly rank smell. From the foliage it spreads to the tubers, which turn brown and fetid.

If blight is spotted, it is best to cut the haulm to the ground immediately and to burn this, lifting the tubers a week or so later. Try and choose dry weather for this, so that mud doesn't stick to them. Vigilant as you may try to be, it is likely that some infected tubers will be stored with the healthy ones, and the disease will continue to spread. So store your crop thinly and go over it fairly frequently until you are certain that no more infected tubers remain.

Blight can be controlled with a copper-based fungicide. These fungicides need to be in contact with the fungus to work, so the haulm has to be well covered. The potato plants themselves are left undamaged, as their protective outer coating prevents the fungicide making contact with their delicate tissue. Whatever spray you apply, its success depends on the application predating the arrival of the first spores. That could, in my area, be in mid-July and I can tell you that it is devilish hard to remember to do the job as early as you should. The weather is dry; the danger seems non-existent. I wait a month, only to discover that I'm too late. This happened year after year with monotonous regularity. Then Perry Rodriguez took over the vegetable-growing and he was determined not to be beaten. He started the protective spraying at the beginning of July and we harvested a marvellous crop that lasted right through to spring.

Perry lifting a root of 'Pink Fir Apple'

IN THE KITCHEN

Collecting the first baskets of potatoes to bring into the kitchen before the crop is lifted is always a thrill. Be sure to dig from well outside each plant. Inadvertently to damage a good tuber is as painful to the lifter as to the lifted.

Skins: what do you do about them? This depends on your attitude. For many people, eating boiled potato skins is a kind of cleansing ritual, stiff with virtue. Skins are good for us; skins make us better. These righteous folk always omit to mention that leaving the skins on is less trouble. Even so, I prefer to remove them. I like the look of skinned potatoes better than that of unskinned and I prefer their taste.

With 'Pink Fir Apple', the shape dictates that you peel after cooking. Any other treatment would be wasteful as well as awkward. I tip the cooked tubers into the kitchen sink; then, with the help of a slowly trickling faucet, peel with my fingers. In really cold weather, I don't even need the water and I almost come to believe that I have at last achieved those asbestos fingers that all my life (until asbestos was decreed wicked) I admired in some of my women friends, who appear to be able to cope equably with temperatures that would make me scream. This peeling really doesn't take long and I can often summon help from understanding friends, if there are many needing attention at the same moment.

Apart from seasoning and melting a little butter over them (and not always that), I serve 'Pink Fir Apple' plain. However, if for a salad, the tubers, after skinning, are immediately cut into narrow rounds and anointed with a vinaigrette dressing (see page 183). The tubers absorb this more efficiently for being hot.

POTATO SALAD WITH WINE AND ANCHOVIES

The large quantity of olive oil (at least half of which deserves to be of the highest quality) means that the pepper and vinegar seasonings need to be fairly generous. Potatoes themselves are, after all, bland. As I do not grow scallions, I substitute a shallot or two, which I find perfectly digestible, even though raw onion gives me trouble.

6 medium (the number depends entirely on
    their size) cooked potatoes, finely sliced
1 bunch scallions
or 1–2 shallots, chopped

Dressing
Salt and crushed or
freshly ground black peppercorns
1 glass red wine
1 tablespoon wine vinegar

1 cup olive oil
1 2oz can of anchovy fillets
A few sprigs each of chervil
    and parsley, chopped

Put the potatoes in a bowl and sprinkle evenly with the scallions or shallots.

In a separate bowl, combine a dash of salt with the crushed peppercorns, wine, wine vinegar and olive oil, mixing well to form a vinaigrette.

Drain and roughly chop the anchovy fillets and mix them into the vinaigrette. Add this and the chopped herbs to the potato mixture, turning the ingredients gently. Marinate for 1 hour at room temperature before serving, or leave for up to 24 hours in the refrigerator.

Jerusalem Artichoke

*T*hat this root vegetable should share the name of artichoke with the globe variety can be put down to a similarity in flavour. This struck me independently of reading it. They are also both promoters of wind, more so in some people than others. As to the Jerusalem part of the name, there are differing theories. It is certainly a corruption of another word.

The plant, in fact, is a sunflower, *Helianthus tuberosus*, from Nova Scotia in Canada, down the east coast of the United States and across to Minnesota in the centre. It grows 7ft or more tall and, right at the end of the season, may reveal its identity by producing some tiny yellow daisies. The leaves are coarse and rough-textured. It is an easily grown and hardy perennial, liable to become a weed if pieces of tuber are left in ground that should have been cleared.

Many gardeners leave a patch of artichokes *in situ* for years on end. This is a great mistake. A new patch should be planted up annually, in early spring and on well-cultivated, well-manured ground. Tubers can be spaced 18in apart, as they make large plants. You also want to bear in mind that they will later cast a lot of shade, which would be deleterious to a low-growing neighbouring crop – leeks, for instance. Ideally, site them either in a group or a row on the northern boundary (southern, in the southern hemisphere) of your vegetable plot.

Jerusalem artichokes in full summer plumage

IN THE KITCHEN

The greatest nuisance, with artichokes, is the knobbliness of their tubers when it comes to cleaning and preparing them. All very well to recommend being extravagant and throwing away the knobs, but that can leave little over. The reason artichokes get into this state is that they have not been replanted. When they have, as I have recommended, the knobs are more like undulations and are easily dealt with, using a knife to pare them. The alternative method of preparation is to parboil them for 10 minutes, run them under a cold tap and then peel them, which is supposed to be quite easy. I do not find it so at all, but try it by all means.

Smooth young Jerusalem artichokes

ARTICHOKE AND CARROT SOUP

As artichokes are so wind-provoking, I like to combine them with carrots, which have a quietening influence and anyway ensure a beautiful colour. Makes 6 to 8 servings.

1½lb Jerusalem artichokes
1 small celeriac *or* a few
sticks of celery
1lb mature carrots
1 small onion
3oz butter
6 cups light stock (see page 13), heated
Salt, freshly ground black pepper
Croûtons of bread fried in butter

Peel the artichokes, discarding their knobs. Slice them into a bowl of water with a few drops of malt vinegar or lemon juice, to prevent discoloration. Peel the celeriac, dice it into fair-sized chunks and let it join the artichokes. Scrape and slice the carrots. Chop the onion finely.

Melt the butter in a capacious saucepan and, lid on, cook the onion gently for 5 minutes. Add the 3 roots and allow them to sweat for a further 10 minutes, together with salt. Now add the stock and simmer for 15 to 20 minutes, until the vegetables are soft. Put through the blender, but not for so long as to lose all texture. Add pepper to taste. Stir and reheat. Serve with the croûtons.

JERUSALEM ARTICHOKE AND SHRIMP SALAD

One of my favourite shellfish recipes from Jane Grigson's *Fish Cookery*. It serves 6 as an appetizer, though it makes a satisfying single-course meal for 2.

2lb Jerusalem artichokes
Vinaigrette dressing made
with good olive oil (see page 183)
Chopped fresh parsley
1lb cooked shrimp in their shells
(better flavoured than ready-shelled
frozen shrimp)

Scrub and peel the artichokes and cook them in boiling salted water for about 15 minutes, until just tender.

Meanwhile, mix the vinaigrette in a large bowl, seasoning it with salt and pepper, a little sugar and a nice dollop of French or German mustard. Put the cooked artichokes, while still warm, into the vinaigrette, cutting them into pieces. When cool, arrange on a shallow dish and sprinkle with plenty of parsley. Arrange the shelled shrimp on top, keeping one or two in their armour as garnish. Serve chilled.

Parsnip

Most European countries other than Britain look down on parsnips as being fit only for animal fodder. A Dutch friend tells me that during times of war and siege, parsnips, with their rich store of sugar and starch, were the only peasant food available. In better times they were rejected for snobbish reasons. For similar reasons they were superseded as staple diet when potatoes became important.

All my friends, British or foreign, seem to enjoy parsnips, so perhaps it is a matter of presentation. They certainly have a strong and individual flavour and their sweetness is astonishing.

Parsnips are, like carrots, biennials of the parsley family, Umbelliferae, and they are prolific in the wild on chalky soils. You see them in yellow flower, along roadside verges, in early summer. In some people and if there is much ultra-violet light about, contact with the growing plant can cause serious blistering and skin rashes.

Because of their long roots, they should be grown on deeply cultivated soil, but it is also sensible, I think, unless you have your eye on the show bench, to grow comparatively short, broad-rooted varieties, which are best designed to make use of top soil and are also easiest to lift, at maturity, without damaging the roots.

Sow in quiet weather (otherwise the winged seeds take off) in late April or early May. It pays to leave

LEFT *Fergus lifting a parsnip at the end of their season, in early spring*
RIGHT *A young parsnip root, just lifted*

118

sowing this late to minimize damage from canker which, with its brown patches, is liable to disfigure parsnip roots. Thin the seedlings to 12in apart. Parsnips are very hardy and taste their best if lifted, throughout the winter, as required. As growth is renewed in early spring, the core of the root toughens and hardens. You may still be able to use the outer part of the root, for a while.

IN THE KITCHEN

The parsnip stem and foliage are set in a deep hollow at the top of the root, and this needs excavating with the tip of a strong knife. The skin must also be removed – easily accomplished with a vegetable peeler. If you cook first and then peel, more of the parsnip's flavour will be retained. Not that I do. The tips of parsnip roots can usefully take their place beneath a roasting joint, to add flavour to subsequent gravy, together with onion, celeriac, carrot and turnip.

ROAST PARSNIPS AND POTATOES

Roast parsnips and potatoes go so well with any roast joint. The difficulty is that the vegetables should be roasted in a very hot oven (220°–230°C/425°–450°F/ gas mark 7–8), but by the time they go in, towards the end of the joint's cooking time, the meat needs a lower temperature (180°C/350°F/gas mark 4, or less). There are various ways of dealing with this.

(1) If you have a double oven, no problem: meat and vegetables can be cooked separately, each at the appropriate temperature.

(2) In a conventional oven, hotter at the top than the bottom, you can move the meat to the lowest shelf before you turn the heat up and put the vegetables in at the top.

(3) In a fan oven, with even heat throughout, you have to cook the vegetables at a lower temperature to start with, so as not to spoil the meat, but you can turn

the temperature up when the meat is taken out to rest.

Whatever your oven arrangements, parboil the vegetables, parsnips for 2 or 3 minutes, potatoes for 5 minutes, before adding them to the hot fat. Use lamb, beef or pork fat, according to the joint, or, most delicious, duck or goose fat. I save the fats from former roastings, ready to use in the larder.

Preheat the fat in a pan, add the parsnips and potatoes, turning them so as to be well coated with fat, and slide the pan into the oven, about half an hour before the meat has finished cooking.

When you take the meat out of the oven, leave it to rest for 15–20 minutes while the parsnips and potatoes complete their cooking and you make the gravy and deal with any green vegetable.

'And suppose I should like to be enjoying my pre-prandial drink in relaxation with my family and guests?' did you ask? Well, I abhor the practice of keeping food hot and waiting. This small sacrifice is worthwhile. There'll be other dishes, on other occasions, that can be prepared beforehand and just finished off at the end.

PARSNIP SOUP 1

Parsnips can seem disconcertingly sweet, in soups. Here this is mitigated by the sharpness of cooking apples. It serves 6 to 8.

1 onion, sliced
2 tablespoons butter, or butter and olive oil
2 large parsnips peeled and diced
3 cooking apples (I use 'Bramley's'), peeled, cored and sliced
5 cups hot chicken stock (see page 13)
1 tablespoon Dijon mustard
Salt, pepper
4 tablespoons heavy cream
Croûtons of bread fried in butter

Soften the onion in the butter; add the parsnips and the apples, and sweat them for a few minutes. Add the hot chicken stock and boil gently for 20 minutes or so, till all are soft. Add the seasonings. Blend in a blender or food processor, though not for so long that all texture is lost. Return to the pan, reheat, check the seasoning and stir in the cream just before serving, along with the croûtons.

If too thick, the soup can be diluted with water.

PARSNIP SOUP 2

This is Jane Grigson's *Curried Parsnip Soup* from *Good Things*. Serves 6 to 8.

1 large parsnip, peeled and sliced
1 cup chopped onion
1 clove garlic, crushed
6 tablespoons butter
1 tablespoon all-purpose flour
1 rounded teaspoon curry powder
5 cups hot beef or chicken stock (see page 13)
Salt, pepper
⅔ cup heavy cream
Chopped chives
Croûtons of bread fried in butter and oil

Put the parsnip, onion and garlic into a heavy saucepan with the butter and cook slowly, covered, for 10 minutes. The vegetables must not brown, but gently absorb the butter. Stir in flour and curry powder to take up the fat, then gradually incorporate the hot stock. Simmer until the parsnip is tender. Liquidize or push through a *mouli-légumes*. Return to the pan, correct the seasoning with salt, pepper and a little more curry powder if liked (but be cautious: keep the flavour mild). Add the cream and a sprinkling of chopped chives. Serve with croûtons.

I may add that chives will not be available from the garden in the early part of the winter but, if reasonably mild, the delicious fresh young tips from new growth will be usable from the end of January on.

121

Celeriac

*T*he distinctive flavour of celery is essential in cookery. However, I do not grow the typical vegetable, whose stems we eat, because on my heavy soil it is a martyr to slug damage.

Instead I grow celeriac, which is the turnip-rooted version. That has a limited season, being at its best all autumn and into early winter. If you're lucky with the weather, it will last till spring. Hard, or even moderate, frost ruins the roots or at the least their top, exposed portion. Nowadays, we protect the plants *in situ*, whenever sharp frost threatens, with a double layer of burlap. If it continues frosty by day, the burlap can remain in position for quite a while without harming the plants. In this way, we extend our cropping season well into February. You can store roots such as these, in damp sand, in a cold yet frost-free place, but I never think they taste as good as when lifted straight from the ground.

Leaves and stems of the herb lovage (see pages 239–40) are my substitute for the flavour of celery in soups and stocks from spring on. The leaves and stems of celeriac itself admirably fulfil this function during their season, as also to include in any *bouquet garni*.

Celeriac should be given a long growing season and plenty of irrigation, if you can manage it, during droughty spells. Even as you handle it, the seed smells powerfully of celery. Sow in a pot in March. The seed will germinate well in a snug cold frame, though it is slow in the early stages. There's always more seed than you need, so resist the temptation to sow thickly just because the seed is there.

LEFT *A young celeriac plant*
RIGHT *A celeriac root that has just been lifted*

When the seedlings are large enough to handle but not yet crowded in their pot, prick them out into a standard seed tray at an 8 x 5 spacing. I need 80 plants to satisfy my greed, so it's two trays for me. Harden them off completely and line the plants out at 1ft spacing in June. The ground they go into needs to be the best: well dug and manured the previous autumn. Otherwise, this is an undemanding crop and the pests and diseases that attack it have never been so serious as to seem to warrant control. If you give the plants what they need culturally, they'll cope without further assistance.

When preparing celeriac, wash the roots and then cut off the foliage before bringing into the kitchen.

IN THE KITCHEN

With a sharp knife, cut off quite a thick layer from the base of the root – enough to leave a clean, white surface, not a surface veined with mud-filled channels between smaller roots. Now, with the same sharp knife, peel from the bottom upwards, going in a spiral around and around the root's perimeter. Rinse it; then chop down on to a board, making parallel sections ½in thick. Now chop at right angles so as to end up with 1in cubes, or rather larger.

You'll find that there's usually, at least in large roots, a hollow central area surrounded by pulp. This doesn't really matter, though I feel it to be a cheat and a sign of bad breeding. I have never found this trait to be more nor less prevalent in different named varieties.

The flesh discolours quickly, so the pieces go straight into salted cold water with a few drops of malt vinegar or lemon juice added.

This is one of my favourite vegetables to accompany almost any meat or fish. Boil for 10 minutes, drain, add a generous knob of butter to the pan and continue cooking at a low heat for another 5 minutes or so.

CELERIAC AND POTATO MASH

This goes well with gamy flavours, such as venison, hare or pheasant.

Cook a large root of celeriac as above. In a separate pan, boil about one-third the quantity of potato. Mash the two together and beat with a large fork, adding season-ing (salt, pepper and nutmeg), chopped parsley and chervil, more butter and soured cream (if the mixture is stiff). Reheat in a *bain-marie*.

See also *Carrot and Celeriac au Gratin* (page 104).

124

Leek

I feel deprived if we are short of leeks. It is the winter vegetable *par excellence*; I don't want to touch it until November, but I expect it to last me into April. It is the hardiest of vegetables and, in my part of the country, can be dug in almost all weathers, the frost seldom penetrating so deep as to prevent this. Careless digging, causing damage to the stem, is extremely annoying, most of all if you yourself are to blame.

Leeks sometimes run to flower long before they should. This may be on account of the weather or it may be due to a badly selected strain. Eventually it is unavoidable, occurring at the end of the leek season. As soon as you spot the trouble, lift the plant that is bolting, slice it to the centre, longitudinally, and extract the flower stem. The rest of the leek will still be tender.

With their lush, glaucous foliage, leeks are a beautiful crop, and they are also imposing in flower, their large, globular heads drying well. They should be grown in ground that was well dug and manured with garden compost or farmyard manure the previous autumn. You want to choose a variety that makes stems of moderate size; these will not be coarse-textured. (Leeks grown for exhibition are another story altogether, eating them not being the main object or even any object.) I am currently growing and getting good results from 'Cortina', which is a late developer. But it is a mistake necessarily to remain faithful to a name through the years. When first released from the breeders, a

*Young leeks before earthing up
in their trench*

Fergus trimming a leek after lifting

variety will have many virtues, but over the years, the actual growers of seed will often be lax on selection and roguing, frequently growing the plants in a climate that is suitable for seed production (leeks ripen very late in Britain, so our climate is unsuitable for this), but useless for spotting defects such as a tendency to bolt. Thus the strain will gradually deteriorate.

I sow my seed in early April, thinly, in 6in pots, germinating them in a cold frame. The seedlings remain in these pots until we are ready to plant them out, in June, by which time they are easily handled and can be dropped into holes made with a dibber. We grow them in a trench, in a double, staggered, row, with about 9in between plants (too close, really).

During their growing season, the young leeks are earthed up. It is very important that this should be done carefully by two people, one of them holding the plants' foliage together while the other shovels the earth thrown up for the trench around their stems. If soil gets in between the leaf bases at this stage, there it will remain and be a great nuisance when you come to prepare the leeks for cooking. Some gardeners simply dibble the seedlings into prepared ground, without making a trench, but the satisfaction of a long white stem at harvesting is partially denied them.

When lifting leeks for the kitchen, make a clean horizontal cut that will remove all the greenery, bar an inch or so. Also remove most of the roots, but leave the basal root plate for the cook to deal with at the last moment.

IN THE KITCHEN

Some of the outer leaves may have been removed when the leeks were lifted and rinsed, but another may need to be peeled off. Trim the top again and the base, so that all trace of root is removed. Now make two lengthways incisions, with the tip of a knife, into the top 3in or so of the leek, opposite to one another. Under a running faucet, part the leaves so released and wash out the dirt. If any remains, it will reveal itself as a dark patch beneath the white skin. Careful washing at this stage is all-important. Before you tell me that you'll buy your dirt-free leeks from the supermarket, after all, and save yourself much trouble, let me beg you to compare the flavour of a home-grown leek with the sanitized, mass-produced equivalent.

If the leeks are simply to be used as a vegetable to go, among others, with meat or fish, I cut them across into lengths of up to 2in, place them in a perforated, adjustable steaming basket and steam them for 10 minutes over boiling water. The flavour of leeks should be mild, though distinct, and needs to be preserved, as does some texture. They want cooking but not reducing to a complete mush. Steaming allows complete control over the cooking period. This will be rather more than 10 minutes if there is more than one layer of leek chunks in the steaming basket.

If leeks are to be served in a composite dish, their mild flavour suggests that one or more of the other ingredients should taste strong – it might be grated Parmesan or smoked bacon bits.

LEEK AND MUSHROOM TART

Adapted from a recipe Jane Grigson had from a Cambridge friend, this is one of my mainstay winter lunch offerings when I have one or two guests and want to get most of the preparation done in advance (it will serve 4). If they are vegetarian, I use only margarine for the pastry fat and leave out the bacon bits, but these last do pep up the flavours wonderfully.

12oz prepared leeks
1½ quantities piecrust dough (see page 12)
1 onion, finely chopped

Butter and oil
3 or 4 smoked bacon slices
¾ cup sliced mushrooms
Salt, pepper
1 extra-large egg *and* 1 extra-large egg yolk
⅔ cup light or whipping cream

Roll out the dough and use it to line an 8–9in tart pan. Leave to rest in the refrigerator or a cool place for 30 minutes.

Place a baking sheet in the oven and preheat to 180°C/350°F/gas mark 4. Prebake the tart shell for 15 minutes.

Meanwhile, prepare the filling. Slice the leeks twice lengthways, the second cut at right angles to the first; then across, into 2in lengths. Stew them with the onion in a little butter and oil until they are soft. There'll be a lot of moisture, so get rid of some of this by leaving the pan lid off towards the end of cooking. Season. If you are using bacon, cut the slices across into ¼in strips and fry. Cook the mushrooms in a little butter in a separate pan, lid off, allowing moisture reduction. Season these (allow plenty of freshly ground black pepper) and add to the pan with the cooked leeks and the fried bacon bits. Allow to cool (this can be done hours in advance).

Beat together the whole egg, the yolk and the cream, then mix into the other ingredients and spread over the tart shell. Put back on the baking sheet and bake at the same temperature for 35–40 minutes. When puffed up and brown on top, the filling is cooked. Serve warm (preferably not reheated) with a crisp green salad.

For the salad, I may buy in an 'Iceberg' lettuce and Florence fennel, but otherwise the ingredients will be home-grown, with various endives (green, coloured, blanched and forced), chervil and, if not frosted, arugula and 'Mega Cress' (see page 194).

LEEK PIE

Jane Grigson's version in *English Food* of a traditional northwest European dish. It seems to me that the excitement in this recipe depends on the quality of the bacon. The leeks, necessarily cooked to a mush, are mildly flavoured.

1lb piecrust dough (see page 12)
1 onion, sliced
1lb leeks, prepared and sliced
3 tablespoons butter
4oz back bacon slices, cut into ¼in strips
1 teaspoon all-purpose flour
½ cup heavy cream
Salt and pepper
A little beaten egg to glaze

Roll out just over half the dough and use it to line an 8–9in tart pan. Leave to rest in the refrigerator or a cool place for 30 minutes.

Meanwhile, prepare the filling. Cook the onion gently in half the butter in a deep skillet. When soft and golden, add the leeks (there should be about 2½ cups of them after trimming) and the remaining butter. Continue to cook slowly until the leeks are reduced to a soft mass. Take the pan off the heat and add the bacon. Mix the flour with the cream and beat the mixture into the leeks so that everything is smoothly amalgamated. Season.

Place a baking sheet in the oven and preheat to 180°C/350°F/gas mark 4. Roll out the remaining dough to make a lid. Put the filling into the pie shell, brush the rim with a little beaten egg and cover with the dough lid. Decorate in a restrained manner and brush over the top with beaten egg. Make a vent-hole in the centre. Bake for 40 to 45 minutes, so that the piecrust is nicely browned.

CHICKEN AND LEEK PIE

This Welsh dish, devised, no doubt, where there were fowls running around, would be excellent with a boiling fowl that needs a couple of hours' stewing. Such fowls have maximum flavour. Unfortunately, they are nowadays rare and hard to come by. The usual forced roasting chickens have little flavour and the flavour of leeks themselves is not strong.

1 boiling or roasting fowl
1 onion, left whole
2 tablespoons chopped celery
or slices of celeriac
Bouquet garni (see page 230)
Salt and pepper
6 prepared leeks
4oz cooked, sliced tongue
2 tablespoons chopped fresh parsley
Chicken stock (see page 13), heated
Double quantity piecrust dough
(see page 12)
A little beaten egg to glaze

Put the chicken into a deep saucepan with the onion, celery (or celeriac), *bouquet garni* and seasonings. Add enough water barely to cover. Simmer until the chicken is tender and cooked through. If you are using a roasting chicken, test after about an hour to see if it is done: push a skewer into the thickest part of the thigh; if the juices run clear the bird is cooked. Older fowl would have clear juices after the same cooking time but will need up to an hour more to become tender. Remove the pan from the heat and leave the contents to cool (you can leave to become quite cold). Cut the chicken off the bones and into convenient pieces. Skim the fat from the stock.

Slice the leeks and blanch in boiling, salted water for 2 minutes. This reduces their bulk and makes them easier to handle. Drain them well. Arrange the chicken and tongue slices in a pie dish. Add the leeks, with the parsley, to the chicken and tongue. Season. Add enough stock to come within 1in of the rim of a deep oval baking dish.

Roll out the dough. Cut a strip from its margin and place around the rim of the pie dish. Brush it with beaten egg and lay the main part of the dough over the pie to make a lid. Knock up the edges, trim off the surplus dough and decorate the pie top with this if you feel artistic. Brush everything over with beaten egg. Slash a venthole to allow steam to escape. Bake in an oven preheated to 180°C/350°F/gas mark 4 for 40 to 45 minutes, until the piecrust is a nice brown.

Shallot and Garlic

S hallots are the only kind of onion that I grow (unless you count chives). I see little point in the home-grown onion. Those on sale are as good and may have better keeping qualities, having been grown where summers are warmer and more ripening. Your own crop is expected to last six or nine months and there will be many losses along the way. Buying them, 2lb at a time, they have little scope for rotting.

Garlic also is always easily purchased, which is what I do, not because I wouldn't like to grow it but because it hates my heavy soil. On light ground you can plant the cloves 6in apart, when the ground begins to work well in early spring – or even in autumn, if your soil is lighter still.

But shallots are not so readily come by on the market. They have their own special flavours and I do not find them indigestible raw, as I unfortunately do onions. Traditionally, shallots are planted on the shortest day and harvested on the longest. Delay those dates by a couple of months and you're nearer the mark. They like light, well-drained soil. My heavy soil is another reason for not planting till it has had the chance to dry out a bit. The bulbs are simply pushed into the ground 6in apart, so that half remains visible. After this, you need to check frequently that something hasn't subsequently scattered them around – pheasants, perhaps, squirrels or rooks.

You harvest when the foliage is sere. Some strains have the habit of running to flower (bolting), which is a nuisance, as this expenditure of energy leaves little for the bulb. If saving your own bulbs for next year's crop, take them from plants that have shown no inclination to bolt. We store our bulbs on racks in a cool garden shed.

AVOCADO DIP

Into a blender, scoop 2 or 3 ripe avocados, adding 1 shallot (roughly chopped), the juice of half a lemon, Worcestershire sauce to taste, salt, pepper and cayenne pepper or Tabasco. Blend for 30 seconds. Turn out into a shallow bowl (for easy scooping) and serve before the meal with thick crinkle-cut potato chips. This is yummy and it is difficult to stop dipping. (Unfortunately, by the time you buy the chips, they have been chucked around to such an extent that at least half are fragmented.)

SHALLOTS WITH PROSCIUTTO AND PECORINO

Serves 3 as an appetizer.

2 tablespoons extra-virgin olive oil
12oz shallots, peeled and
cut into chunks
Pinch of brown sugar
Pinch of finely chopped thyme leaves
Salt and black pepper
4 tablespoons balsamic vinegar
4oz sliced *prosciutto*
2oz Pecorino cheese (or Parmesan,
if not too hard)

Heat the olive oil in a heavy-based saucepan and stir in the shallots. Cover and sweat over a low heat for 5 minutes. Add the sugar, thyme, salt and pepper, and cook in the shallots' own juices, very gently, for 30 minutes. Remove from the heat, add the vinegar, stir well and allow to cool.

When ready to serve, place some shallots and their own sauce on each plate, lay the *prosciutto* on top, and add shavings of the cheese, using a cheese parer or vegetable peeler.

BRILL WITH VERMOUTH

Chopped shallot makes an admirable bed on which to lay and bake fillets of fish. Jane Grigson gives the following recipe for brill (which I can get, locally caught, in Hastings) in *Fish Cookery*, but it is equally good with turbot, lemon sole or John Dory.

6 large brill fillets
Salt and white pepper
4 tablespoons butter, melted
8 heaped tablespoons soft
white breadcrumbs
3 shallots, finely chopped
1 heaped tablespoon chopped fresh parsley
10 tablespoons dry vermouth
6 tablespoons butter, diced

Preheat the oven to 230°C/450°F/gas mark 8.

Season the fish. Brush it with a little of the melted butter and press it into the breadcrumbs until coated. Lightly grease a baking dish. Place the fillets in it, on top of the shallots and parsley. Pour the vermouth around the sides of the fish. Sprinkle any remaining breadcrumbs on top and pour the rest of the melted butter over them. Bake for about 10 minutes. Put the cooked brill on to a warm dish. Pour the cooking juices into a small pan and whisk in the remaining 6 tablespoons butter. Pour over the fish and serve immediately.

In practice, I find there are no cooking juices, in which case reduce more vermouth in a small pan (to evaporate its alcohol content) and whisk in the butter. On removing the fish from its baking dish, pour and scrape what remains of fluids and solids into the pan and stir before pouring over the fish.

PAGES 134–135 *From each shallot, planted in spring, a cluster of bulbs develops*

GREEN VEGETABLES

Spinach

Fava Beans

Peas

French Beans

Globe Artichoke

Seakale

Cauliflower, Broccoli & Kale

Cabbage

Spinach

There is confusion in the naming of this vegetable. True spinach, *Spinacia oleracea*, grows quickly from seed but also bolts quickly. Spinach beet, *Beta vulgaris* Cicla Group, is passed off as spinach, say in a 'Pick Your Own', but is really a selection of beet in which the root is small but much leaf is produced over a long period without bolting, which is what makes it popular. The flavour is quite different. I do not grow it, though I do, late in the season when their roots are fully grown, cook the young leaves on my beets. But here I write of true spinach.

Well-manured, moist ground best suits this vegetable. If, furthermore, the seedlings are thinned to 6 or 8in, individuals in the row will have the chance to make fine plants with really large leaves. When you consider that from a single picking you may require as much as 4lb of leaf, it is easy to appreciate that good cultivation pays. So does a nice long row.

I do not therefore go along with the customary advice of sowing at fortnightly intervals from spring to high summer. This appears to presume fairly short rows, which are useless where a few keen spinach eaters are gathered together. Better to be able to lash out with long rows, sown three or four times between spring and summer. If a gap develops between harvests, it isn't the end of the world; there are other summer vegetables.

In an open autumn, late sowings in August and September will enable you to pick into November. Then you should leave the plants to overwinter, which they will if the weather is not too severe, cropping again in April. But they hate to be waterlogged, so heavy ground combined with heavy autumn rains are against them. And you must control slug populations.

Spinach leaves are smooth and stiff, always curved – usually convex. Don't send an ignoramus out to pick your spinach for you. Do it yourself, thus saving preparation in the kitchen. Pick the leaf blades, leaving the stems behind. These blades are enormously bulky as well as springy. You need to pick into a large, incurving basket, otherwise they'll jump out again as you put them in. This can also present a problem as you start to cook.

PAGE 136 *Savoy cabbage 'January King'*
PAGE 137 *The globe artichoke 'Gros Vert de Laon'*
OPPOSITE *The foliage of true spinach*

I N   T H E   K I T C H E N

Wash the leaves thoroughly and press as many as you can into a (large) pan. Keep the lid on with a weight. If the pan won't accommodate all the leaves, wait till the first batch has subsided and then add the rest.

You need never add water when cooking spinach. That which hangs about on the leaves after their washing is sufficient, but you want to go easy on the salt, before cooking, as there'll be little water to dilute it. Cook on a low heat at first, till the leaves have started to subside, after which you can turn it up. It can all be done in 10 minutes but, if you're not in a hurry, you can keep the heat low throughout and let it take longer.

I never enjoyed the spinach that was piled into us as children, because it was 'good for us', and I cannot imagine that it was attractively presented; just

a sulky, sodden mess. But it should be a most delicious, tangy vegetable to which no other compares. It leaves a slight roughness on the palate. It is rich in oxalates, which are currently supposed to be 'bad for us', but I have, although a rheumaticky person, noticed no special ill-effects; nor from rhubarb, asparagus, strawberries or gooseberries, all of them warned against for the same reason. After cooking, I drain the spinach and extrude immense quantities of water by pressing hard on it with a pancake turner. The edge of this also breaks the spinach up to a convenient texture.

After as much water as possible has gone, pepper and nutmeg can be added and lots of butter (I attempt compensation by denying myself butter with my bread and marmalade at breakfast).

Spinach reheats well, if necessary. Jane Grigson describes a method whereby, starting with 3–4lb of spinach, you reheat it daily for four days, adding 1 stick of butter each day. She gives many tempting spinach recipes, especially in *Good Things* and the *Vegetable Book*. She rightly emphasizes the importance of contrasting textures and recommends serving spinach (it could make a simple meal) with slices of bread fried in butter or olive oil.

S P I N A C H   T A R T

Serves 2 or 3.

1½ lb spinach
1 quantity piecrust dough (see page 12)
A little egg yolk, to glaze
6 tablespoons butter
Salt and black pepper
Grated nutmeg
1 onion, finely chopped
⅔ cup light or whipping cream
1 extra-large egg
1 extra-large egg yolk
4 slices bacon, cut into small
bits and fried

Roll out the dough and use it to line a 7in tart pan with a removable base. Leave it to rest in the refrigerator or a cool place for 30 minutes.

Place a baking sheet in the oven and preheat to 180°C/350°F/gas mark 4. Pre-bake the tart shell for 15 minutes. Brush with egg yolk and bake for 5 minutes longer.

Cook the spinach (see page 140) and drain. Add 2 tablespoons butter and season with salt and pepper and grated nutmeg. In a small covered saucepan, cook the onion, without browning, in the remaining butter. Beat together the cream, the whole egg and the yolk.

Into the spinach, stir the onion, the fried bacon bits and the egg and cream mixture. Spread this mixture over the pastry. Bake for 35 minutes. Ideally, I think this should be completed half an hour before eating. Serve with a green salad.

D O V E R   S O L E   F L O R E N T I N E

With most Dovers being so small, nowadays, thanks to overfishing, they are hard to fillet and I usually do this dish with two small fish, whole, skinned on the black side. That's for looks; the skin tastes perfectly good.

The Florentine method of combining a cheese sauce with a bed of spinach can be used for other basic ingredients such as fillets of various fish, boiled eggs or slices of cooked ham. It is always stimulating. Serves 2.

2 small Dover soles
Salt and pepper
Half a glass *each* dry white wine
and fish fumet
or 1 glass of dry white wine
Juice of half a lemon
1½lb spinach, cooked and
drained (see page 140)
2 tablespoons butter
1 tablespoon *each* grated Gruyère and
Parmesan cheese, mixed together

Mornay sauce
2 tablespoons butter
1 small onion, chopped
3–4oz mushroom trimmings *or*
mushrooms, chopped
2 tablespoons all-purpose flour
1¼ cups vegetable stock, heated
1¼ cups milk *or* milk and
light cream combined
Salt and pepper
2 tablespoons *each* grated Gruyère and
Parmesan cheeses, mixed together
Grated nutmeg

To make the mornay sauce, melt the butter and sweat the onion in it till it begins to soften. Add the mushrooms, cover the pan and stew for 5 minutes. Stir in the flour and moisten gradually with the stock, then the milk. Simmer the sauce for about 20 minutes, till it is reduced by a third. Season with salt and pepper. Off the heat, stir in the cheeses and a little nutmeg.

Butter a roasting pan. Season the soles, lay them in the buttered pan, and pour over the wine and fish fumet – or wine alone – and the lemon juice. Bake in a pre-heated 180°C/350°F/gas mark 4 oven for 15 minutes, basting from time to time.

Mix the cooked spinach and the butter together with some seasoning, and spread on the bottom of a gratin dish.

Lay the cooked soles on top of the spinach and cover all with mornay sauce. Sprinkle with more grated mixed Gruyère and Parmesan and glaze under a hot broiler.

SPINACH SOUFFLÉ

Serves 2 or 3.

3 tablespoons dry breadcrumbs
1½–2lb spinach
3 tablespoons butter
Salt, pepper
2 tablespoons all-purpose flour
⅔ cup milk
4 or 5 eggs, separated
3 tablespoons grated Parmesan
Grated nutmeg

Optional
1 2oz can of anchovies, chopped
and/or ⅓ cup pine kernels,
lightly browned
or ⅓ cup slivered almonds,
lightly browned, *or* 1 cup diced smoked
cooked ham

Place a baking sheet in the oven and pre-heat to 190°C/375°F/gas mark 5. Butter a 6-cup soufflé dish and line it with bread-crumbs, tilting out and saving the surplus.

Cook and drain the spinach (see page 140), adding 1 tablespoon of the butter and seasoning. Melt the remaining butter, stir in the flour and leave it to cook for a minute. Gradually stir in the milk. Tilt this sauce into your blender together with the spinach, the egg yolks and half the Parmesan. Whiz, but not for so long as to lose all texture.

Turn out into a bowl, adding optional extras at this stage. Stiffly whip the egg whites and fold these in gently. If you go on till the last visible blob of white has gone, there'll be little air left in the mixture and it won't rise far.

Pour the mixture into the soufflé dish and surface it with the remaining cheese and crumbs. Place the dish on the baking sheet. Bake for 40 minutes.

Fava Beans

*I*am as fond of fava beans as of garden-grown peas and they are just as good for freezing, so we grow a large batch. They have a long history in European cultivation, but are regarded in much of France as no better than cattle fodder. Which they are, in a tough, hard-seeded form, and the smell of a bean-field in flower is one of the best.

That is quite a different product from the beans we should be growing for our own consumption. 'Should', I say, because if you buy frozen fava beans they are disappointingly hard and tough, as though cattle had been breathing down the neck of the breeders. Luckily, we can grow the tenderest and tastiest fava beans in our own gardens.

The plants are very hardy and some enthusiasts, gardening on light soil, will even sow in November although, in respect of when the pods are actually ready to pick the following June, there cannot be more than a day or two's advantage over those that are sown in February. On our heavy soil, we sow in the second half of April, which is about as late as it is possible to do so successfully. Any later, and the flowers seem unable to set pods. Our crop comes in in the second half of July, or even in August, in a late season. Before that, I can enjoy someone else's beans by buying from a farm shop. Our local 'Pick Your Own' also has them by late June, though the beans are on the hard side, even when young.

Except for exhibition, I don't think that very large-podded varieties are practical or desirable. Smaller pods will be borne more numerously on the plant and will each contain a larger number of (smaller) beans.

RIGHT *Fava bean plants are still quite short when they flower*
PAGE 144 *Fava beans in flower waft a delicious scent*
PAGE 145 *When they reach this stage, eat a proportion of the beans on each plant, whole*

Currently, I find 'Express' a satisfactory variety. We sow four large packets of fifty beans in each, all in one go, and have a great hulling session when they need freezing (see opposite).

I also like the dwarf fava bean called 'The Sutton'. It crops freely, with small pods, and has the great advantage of not requiring to be staked.

The ground should have been manured and dug the previous autumn. If beans are sown in single rows, a spacing of about 18in between is right. We sow in double rows, which is better, I think, allowing easier movement among the plants when they are tall. In that case, allow a 9–10in space inside each double row, and 30in between them and the next pair. Sow the seed in 3in-deep drills and at a spacing along the row of about 10in. Most varieties require support. Knock stout stakes in at the end of each row (and intermediate stakes if the row is long) and run a length of string around the outside at a height of 30in.

When the plants have flowered and set a crop of small pods, remove the growing tips and cook a dish of them. The reason for pinching them out is that they will otherwise become infested with the bean aphid, a horrible black thing which breeds at an alarming rate. It has an interesting life cycle, spending the early part of the growing season feeding on spindle and viburnum (terrible on *Viburnum carlesii* and *V. opulus*). It then migrates to beans, nasturtiums, dahlias and a number of vegetable crops. It is sensible to spray as soon as the trouble is spotted. In the autumn, the aphid returns to its shrubby hosts and there lays overwintering eggs. In this condition they are well protected against the coldest winter weather, so when you hear that a severe winter must have killed off the pests, don't believe a word of it.

After the young pods have set, be on the watch and make a picking of them, a few from each plant, when about 4in long. This will in no way detract from the weight of the final crop. When the main crop is ready to harvest, timing is all-important. Jane Grigson generally assumes that quite a lot of the beans will have tough skins from having been left on the plant for too long and most of her recipes recommend slipping the beans out of their jackets after cooking. That is tedious, though sometimes necessary towards the end of the crop when you are catching up with pods that were missed earlier. On the whole, vigilance with your own crop will ensure that it will be gathered when the beans are quite small enough not to have hardened skins.

You will soon get the hang of deciding, correctly, at what stage the pod should be picked, without needing to look inside too many examples. It should still be soft and a little squelchy when pressed from opposite sides between fingers and thumb. But you also want to be sure that it is firm enough to have reasonably sized beans within.

I N   T H E   K I T C H E N

Extracting beans from their pods is not nearly as neat an operation as with peas. Your hands will be blackened, unless you wear gloves. Use a knife to run down the length of the bean, on whichever side presents itself the more easily for this operation. The pod will then split open neatly, whereas it will turn clumsily in spirals if you try to tear it apart.

When freezing fava beans, don't try and blanch too many at a time. They lie so densely in the basket that if you have much more than a 3in layer the water for blanching will take a long time to return to the boil. Boil the beans for 2 minutes, plunge them into cold water to cool them quickly, drain, allow to cool, and freeze in plastic bags.

T O   C O O K   Y O U N G   B E A N   P O D S

Selectively pick whole bean pods (see opposite) when only 3–4in long. Boil them whole in salted water for 10 to 15 minutes. Drain and add a good knob of butter. The beans can, if necessary, be broken up at this stage. The flavour is slightly bitter and stimulating.

F A V A   B E A N S   A N D   B A C O N

Fava beans and bacon are made for each other. I buy a 5–6lb piece of smoked ham on the bone from my local butcher. The flavour is incomparably better than any-thing you can obtain from a supermarket. For this quality meat, family butchers badly need our support, as we need them to maintain high standards.

This is a simple meal to organize when I have a large weekend gathering. Often the beans are taken from the freezer.

I soak the smoked ham overnight and bring it to the boil in fresh water from cold; then cook for 2 hours. Towards the end, I remove some of the ham stock to make a parsley sauce, with 4 tablespoons butter, 1/3 cup all-purpose flour and equal quantities of stock and milk. Season and cook down to a reasonably thick sauce, adding plenty of finely chopped parsley leaf (save the stems for flavouring stocks). Boil the beans for 10 to 15 minutes. Mashed potatoes, softened with butter and sour cream, also go well with ham. The meat itself is skinned, at the end of its 2 hours' cooking, and is then ready to be carved.

Peas

What could be more delicious than your own green peas, picked straight from the garden, shucked forthwith, with friends to help – we sit on the terrace, with colanders on our laps for the peas and boxes on the ground for the shucks – and immediately cooked so that there is absolutely no loss of flavour and sweetness? Here is a vegetable which you simply must grow yourself, as there is no adequate substitute.

The peas you constantly meet in restaurants have virtually no original flavour, but a great deal of ersatz sweetening. Calling them *petits pois* decreases their size and increases their price but in no way improves their flavour. Peas and fava beans are the best of all vegetables for freezing from your garden, but the frozen peas you buy, again, taste of artificial sweetening and are poorly flavoured. In large part this is because the commercially grown peas for canning and freezing – they all have to be machine-harvested at once – are poorly flavoured in the first place. I pick peas fresh from our local 'Pick Your Own', before mine are ready. They are enjoyable but at a mediocre level of enjoyment. Flavour has never stood high on the scale of importance in the world of mass production. I prefer to buy snow and sugar snap peas from a local farm shop, now and again. In your own garden they are tyrannical, threatening you with string, obesity and every ugly aspect of middle age that we are only too conscious of in ourselves, without meeting them in our plants – unless they are picked *every* day (like zucchini). Sugar snaps are preferable to snow peas, not being too sweet and cloying, with a leaning towards sliminess. Snow peas have become a cliché in cookery of recent years, on every would-be fashionable restaurant plate.

If you use a deep-freeze, a succession of garden peas is less important than a well-grown, and therefore productive, crop. The only other consideration is the availability of enough willing hands when baskets of peas are ready to be dealt with all at once from the garden. Really, peas, when ready, should not be kept waiting to be picked and immediately seen to, for more than a day.

On our heavy ground, there is no point in aiming for an early crop. Peas can easily rot in the ground, if conditions are too wet or cold, and this is truest of the nicest peas to eat, which are known as marrow fats or wrinkled peas. Wrinkled only when ripe, of course. Rounded peas are hardier and can be sown earlier, but haven't the flavour of wrinkled types.

Peas

So we wait till the end of April, or even early May (depending on the weather) – before making our big sowing. You can go on sowing till mid-June, and we do make at least one later effort (going against what I have just said), but are invariably paid out for our stupidity by running into drought, the plants too small to be worth supporting, and extremely prone to mildew, though we give a protective spraying against that. Well, there's always the chance that things will be better next year.

The ground should have been well prepared and deeply dug in the previous autumn. As the pea moth, which is the cause of maggots in the pods at the time of harvest, pupates close to where the peas are grown, you want to move the site as far as you can, from year to year.

Drills for sowing can either be of the usual V-shape, with a single trickle of seed, or they can be flat-bottomed and 6in wide. In either case, sow about 2in deep and not too thickly. The seedlings should be about 2in apart. They can be thinned, of course.

Support will be needed before the young seedlings are blown sideways. Peasticks (or brushwood), cut from the bushy top growth of such as hazel, hornbeam or birch, are ideal. Otherwise you'll have to make do with netting (not of wire), supported by stakes. The brushwood should be on each side of a broad drill and 4in from it. Top it at the height you expect the peas to reach (about 3ft, with 'Hurst Greenshaft', which is the variety we have been growing for some years). Stick the trimmings in the ground to give the seedlings a hoist on to the brushwood, which will be distinctly thick and stemmy at the base.

Our peas come in at some time in July. The pods, when picked, should be reasonably full but not

RIGHT *The first picking of 'Hurst Greenshaft'*
PAGE 150 *Green peas in flower*
PAGE 151 *These peas will be ready for picking in a few days*

hard, still having a little give in their flanks when pressed laterally, and opening with a pop (like a fuchsia bud) when pressed on the ventral ridge. If there is any wrinkling on the surface of the pod, the contents will be too old and floury for use as a green vegetable.

IN THE KITCHEN

Don't boil peas in too much water as they are (for some reason) very prone to boiling over. Mint is the traditional flavour to cook them with. They shouldn't need boiling for longer than 10 minutes.

DUCK STEWED WITH GREEN PEAS

This is a seasonal recipe from Jane Grigson's *English Food*, which I always look forward to each July. In reproducing it, I give rather shorter cooking times. Serves 4.

Duck weighing about 4–5lb, with giblets
1¼ cups giblet stock (see below)
Bouquet garni (bay leaf, parsley, thyme, savory, tarragon)
1 large lettuce, shredded
1lb shelled peas
Salt and pepper
2 egg yolks
4 tablespoons heavy cream
Lemon juice

Use the duck giblets to make the stock in advance. Put the washed giblets in a pan, with a small onion, halved. Cover with 2½ cups of water and bring to a simmer. Skim, then add a carrot, a celery stalk, a glass of wine, herbs, and seasoning. Half-cover the pan and simmer for 1½–2 hours. Strain, then boil down to 1¼ cups.

Prick the duck all over with a fork, and tuck the *bouquet garni* into the cavity. Brown it all over in a little oil, in a casserole – do this slowly so that the fat has a chance to run out. Pour this off and save for another occasion, for roasting potatoes and parsnips. Position the duck breast down and pour over the stock. Cover and cook in the oven for 1 hour, at 150°C/300°F/gas mark 2.

Turn the duck over. Add the lettuce and peas and some seasoning. Replace the cover and complete the cooking – another half hour. Take out the duck, peas and lettuce (drained), and keep them warm while the sauce is finished.

If necessary, boil the stock down hard for 5 minutes to concentrate the flavour. Mix the yolks and cream in a bowl and whisk in about half the stock. Return this to the cooking pot set over a low heat (it will curdle if allowed to boil). Finish with lemon juice and seasoning.

My own method is then to carve and serve the duck and vegetables in the kitchen, and to spoon the sauce straight from the casserole on to each plate.

French Beans

*D*warf French beans (which Americans call snap beans) are the only kind I grow (apart from the quite different fava bean). Unlike the majority of my compatriots, I am none too fond of runner beans and I gave up growing them quite a while back. I find their texture unpleasing and their flavour slightly rancid. Being very long, they are normally sliced into quite small pieces, which means that most of the flavour is lost in the cooking water and what remains tastes of the knife. It was quite a relief to read that Jane Grigson did not much care for the scarlet runner. In flower, of course (unless you are so cranky as to grow a dirty white-flowered variety) it is ornamental.

But the dwarf French kinds are a delight and so good served on their own, with just a few extra embellishments, that one begins to understand why the French and Italians habitually make a separate dish of any vegetable, rather than serving them all concurrently with fish or meat.

As regards varieties, new ones keep coming along and I am happy to give them a trial, though 'Tendergreen' and 'Radar' are two from which I am currently getting satisfaction. The main points to look out for are stringlessness and prolonged cropping. The latter can only be achieved if pods are removed from the plant as soon as ready for picking. This will stimulate renewed flowering and the production of later pods.

French beans are quite tender plants and the soil needs to have warmed up before they are sown. On our heavy fare, this means that we quite normally delay a first sowing till the end of May, although a heatwave earlier in the month tempts us to sow then.

The ground will have been dug and manured in the previous autumn or winter. Drills are drawn out 2ft apart and the beans sown 2in deep at a spacing of 9in. A second sowing, in late June or early July, will keep us in young pods till October, but may run into drought difficulties. However, the precaution of watering the bottom of the drill before sowing will often get germination started.

I enjoy picking beans. As I hate stooping, I kneel, and the ground is often so dry that a kneeling mat is unnecessary. To save time and trouble in the kitchen, I pick each bean by pressing and bending it between thumb and fingers, just below the top. The beans are then laid in the basket, pointing in the same direction. All that is then necessary by way of preparation in the kitchen

Newly picked French beans; the tops have been left on the plants

is removal of the 'tail', with a sharp knife. The pods are then washed. I prefer to retain all their flavour by cooking them whole, but if they need to be shortened, I snap them in half.

COOKING FRENCH BEANS

The fashion for undercooking beans and serving them virtually raw has spread like a virus into every restaurant and many homes. This is supposed to be chic, but ill serves the purpose of cooking, which is to bring out the flavour of whatever is being cooked. At a rolling boil, and with the saucepan lid off (to retain a good colour), cook your beans for 10 minutes. This will leave them with quite sufficient texture to preserve a crunch between the molars, and the flavour will be there.

After draining the beans, they need to be given a shine with melted butter or olive oil. Seasoning is added. Or, in a separate pan, you can melt some butter and slowly, at a low temperature, soften a shallot and small clove of garlic, both finely chopped together. Stir into the beans and add chopped parsley.

Globe Artichoke

The globe artichoke, *Cynara scolymus*, does not really deserve specific rank, having been developed from the cardoon, *C. cardunculus*, a much taller plant with violently prickly flower heads that do not at all lend themselves to handling at table, although their young stems can be blanched for eating like celery. I have never tried this out. But cardoons are handsome plants in a border setting, which is their place in the garden.

I have a passion for globe artichokes and grow a great many plants, but it has to be admitted that this crop is wasteful of space, if space is at a premium. The wonderful grey, dissected foliage and generally handsome appearance right up to the time of being ready to eat sometimes tempts those who haven't much space to spare to include them in their flower border. However, once you have cut the heads to eat, the plant never looks the same again and nothing will disguise the fact. From early June on, you are the owner of an eyesore. Other gardeners try to save on space by close planting. This doesn't work either, the result being blind, non-productive plants. They really need to be set a full 3ft apart. In their first year they will (if you do as I say) produce single crowns, which is fine. In subsequent years, there will be multiple crowns attended by the danger that they will spoil one another by overcrowding. So, from the spring of the second year on, you should, with a strong pruning knife, cut out all the crowns but three, on every plant,

Artichokes are long-lived perennials, but young stock is the most productive. I generally keep mine for two years only, three at most. With good management, you should have artichokes to cut from May till the first frosts, though there may be small gaps in continuity.

It is most important to start with good stock of an accredited named variety that has been vegetatively propagated. Artichokes are easily raised from seed but the resulting seedlings are always inferior to named clones. For one thing they are often uncomfortably prickly, which is quite unnecessary; or the crowns will not be as large and succulent as is desirable. There is a purple-tinted artichoke which I particularly abhor. Avoid it. When buying 'rooted off-sets', as the slips that are sent you are generally known, make sure that you are buying vegetatively raised stock.

The two varieties that I grow are 'Gros Camus de Bretagne' and 'Gros Vert de Laon'. The former is shaped like a football, several together fitting more easily into a (large) saucepan than the latter, which has outward-pointing scales. The Breton is slightly weaker-stemmed, and may take on a recumbent position, which doesn't really matter, but it is also slightly the less hardy. In Sussex I never protect my stock, but losses do sometimes have to be made good after a hard winter. I find that 'Gros Camus de Bretagne' has more succulent scale bases than 'Gros Vert de Laon' and I grow double the quantity of it. However, 'Gros Vert de Laon' is the more productive and should not be discounted. I am not familiar with 'Green Globe'.

CULTIVATING ARTICHOKES

Artichokes should be planted on well-manured, fertile ground. Here, April is generally a good month. The slips used are severed from the main stem, below ground level, at that point where shoot meets trunk, so to speak. If you use a sharp knife for this operation, there'll be no need for further trimming, except for shortening the foliage, with one determined cross-cut made about half-way down the shoot. Above the point where you severed the offset from the plant, there will usually (not always), be incipient young roots showing. Even if there aren't, this basal part should be firm and slightly swollen. Do not on any account take rooted offsets with multiple shoots; just the one snout per offset.

Make sure your slips don't dry out before you dibble and water them in, and don't choose a day of drying winds and scorching sunshine. You'll need to follow up with a watering can on future days, as you see the need, until it becomes clear that your slips have become plants and that each has made a new leaf.

We find, in the south of England, that offsets planted in April will be cropping from July on – mostly in July and August. But as some plants develop more slowly than others, the later ones will crop in September–October and the weaklings, not till the next year. These second-season plants will start cropping late in May (unless the season is backward) and will be at their peak in June before falling off in July, which is just when the next young bed will be getting into its stride, providing continuity of cropping.

It is possible to make your new bed too early. If established in March, its first cropping may start at the end of June, overlapping the second-year bed by too wide a margin. (For heaven's sake don't go on holiday in June.)

When the bed has cropped a second time, it can be scrapped in July in time for late crops of lettuce, Florence fennel, radish, arugula and the like. Or you may keep it for a third year. In its third spring, the plants will provide ideal propagating material for a new bed.

It is perfectly possible to take rooted offsets at any time during the summer. In cold areas, July would be a good time, potting up the offsets, keeping the young plants under glass for the winter and setting them out the following May.

The only serious pest of artichokes is black aphids, which make a horrible mess of developing globes, getting right down into and between the scales. You must resort to an aphicide. Earwigs are the other, not too serious, problem. They use the gaps between scales as a daytime dormitory. I always pick the artichokes with enough stem to hold them by, comfortably; then beat a couple of heads together, turning them around as I do so. This vibration dislodges the earwigs, which will then fall to the ground. You may have to do this over the kitchen sink, chasing the earwigs around its slippery sides.

HARVESTING

Artichokes are nowadays on offer in all the larger stores, but I am always impressed by their wizened appearance compared with the fresh product straight from my own garden. Flavour goes hand-in-hand with appearance.

From a strong crown, one central globe will be produced together with at least two, later developing and smaller, side globes; sometimes three, four or even five of these. The temptation, which I seldom resist, is to eat the central globe, as soon as ready, and to allow the laterals to develop till they, too, are ready for the normal kitchen treatment. However, as with the cultivation of prize dahlias, you can go all out for the largest central globe obtainable, in which case the side-shoots will be removed at an early stage. But even at this stage, they will be fit for eating – whole; or, if some parts have toughened, for eating whole after removal of the tough parts of the outer scales. When I can see a large crop in the offing, I indulge in salads that I make with these undeveloped side globes (see page 161).

I normally eat my artichokes in a more mature condition, simply boiling them for 40 minutes (they take longer to cook than you might expect) and eating them with pepper and salt and some melted butter on the side of my plate.

Globe artichoke 'Gros Vert de Laon'

Drain the artichokes well, after boiling, otherwise water will dilute the butter.

When the heads are sizeable but still young, there will be very little fibre in the stem beneath, and this should be eaten. It is a little more bitter than the artichoke bottom itself, but no less delicious for that. When maturer heads are being dealt with, the stem should be severed from the head as close to it as you can cut.

While eating a boiled artichoke, discard the lowest, smallest outer scales. Proceeding inwards, you come to the fattest and most succulent scale bases, which are dipped individually into salt and pepper and butter, before being dragged into your mouth with the front incisors. As you reach thinner scales, several can be dealt with together. It is a little unfair, it seems to me, that, like the Earth, artichokes become hotter as you near the centre. The final cone of purple-tipped scales should be removed in one, thus revealing the hairy choke, which would be the flower's stamens. Peel these off with a spoon and you are left with the most ambrosial part of all, the thick, saucer-shaped artichoke bottom.

With elderly artichokes that you didn't get around to cutting as soon as you should, the bottoms will still remain tender and succulent when the rest is not. After boiling in the usual way, dismember the flowers to leave just the bottoms. Chop them up a little and cover with scrambled egg, seasoned to taste – salt, pepper, Dijon mustard, chopped chives, parsley. Scrambled egg has the best flavour when very little milk is used (otherwise it becomes a sloppy custard) and it is cooked slowly (but not for too long) over a *bain-marie*.

ATTITUDES TO ARTICHOKES

If you are brought up with artichokes from the first, there is no difficulty about adjusting to the rather peculiar method of eating them. I can, and do, eat them every day, if I am on my own and they are asking to be eaten. I never tire of them. My brother, Oliver, had a surfeit when young and didn't want to see them again until near the end of his life. I never saw my father (who died when I was twelve) eat them, and he expressed mock horror when his children were indulging in the even more bestial ritual of guzzling corn on the cob. He would hold a napkin up in front of his eyes. It must have been my mother who brought artichokes to Dixter, but when she developed a taste for them, I do not know.

I entertain a good deal. Nearly all my young friends are adaptable and, if they have not met artichokes before meeting me, it takes them little or no time to get the hang of them. There are various short cuts which allow their consumption to be quite rapid, though never as quick as mine, but then that gives me time to get ready for the main course. However, there are stuffier adults who are nervous of and unfamiliar with artichokes but don't like to admit it. (Advice on how to tackle them is easily forthcoming and seldom has to come from me.) They pretend that they are a lot of fuss about nothing. The worst so far was an American, Paul Aden, who, after pulling his artichoke to pieces, left it all on his plate. 'Are you going to eat it?' I inquired, wondering if he was just resting. 'I have had sufficient,' he replied loftily.

I thought a couple of kids who'd never seen artichokes would not be attracted, as children are often suspicious of what they don't know, especially if their parents encourage them to be picky. So I only helped them to the grown-ups. But the two youngsters hung around their parents' plates and insisted on joining in. They were easy converts.

A R T I C H O K E   S A L A D

Take a dozen very small, young artichokes. A few inches of stem can be left but any tough parts of the scales must be removed with a sharp knife. Cut into quarters and drop into a bowl of water to prevent discoloration (a few drops of vinegar will assist). Then put them into a large skillet with 6 tablespoons of good olive oil and enough boiling water barely to cover. Add salt and a dozen roughly crushed peppercorns.

Boil till all the water has evaporated and add the juice of a lemon. Serve cold (or hot, if you prefer) with a coating of chopped parsley.

Seakale

*A*s a plant, seakale is as beautiful as any vegetable we grow. It is a native around our coasts, found in shingle just above the tide line and so near to the sea as to experience little competition from other plants. On first appearing in spring, the crinkly leaves are purple, later becoming glaucous on account of the waxy coating that protects them from the extreme exposure of their habitat. The cruciferous white flowers are borne in dense bouquets, wafting on the air the scent of honey. They open in May, those nearest to the reflected warmth of the surrounding shingle, which they tend to hug, expanding first. There follows a heavy crop of oval seedpods.

As an ornamental, seakale is an excellent edge-of-border ingredient, especially in a white garden, where its contribution as a foliage feature is prolonged by cutting everything to the ground immediately after flowering, whereupon a new crop of leaves is quickly put forth. The chief snag in late summer is decimation by Cabbage White caterpillars, for this is a member of the cabbage family. You need to be on the watch for incipient damage. Often you can squash the clusters of pale yellow eggs of the Large White butterfly, before they have even hatched. Look on the leaves' undersides.

The seedheads would be a handsome garden feature if seed were set. Most gardeners, however, reproduce their seakale vegetatively, from root cuttings. But cross-pollination is needed if seed is to be set. The way round this, of course, is to grow a batch of seakale from seed, which is on the market. All your plants will then be genetically different. The resulting plants will provide edible shoots within two seasons, but there is liable to be some variation in quality and performance. By and large, vegetable gardeners prefer uniformity, so they keep to one clone. This has another advantage, inasmuch as seakale propagated from root cuttings will produce a crop within only one year.

If you grow from seed sown in spring, line the seedlings out for the summer at a fairly close spacing of 9in or so, and replant them in well prepared ground, 15in apart, the next spring. When gardeners interested in ecology study natural habitats, they often make the mistake of thinking that these should, as far as possible, be replicated in the garden. The starvation diet that keeps all competitors at bay in the wild is not a garden situation. We can keep

Seakale flowering in a border setting

competitive weeds at bay for the seakale, ourselves. A rich diet combined with good drainage will result in a far larger crop.

Grown from 'thongs' (roots), seakale is lifted in the autumn and side-roots 'the thickness of a pencil' (the traditional description) are cut off, each 6in or so long. You need to remember which is the top of the root and which the bottom. As there may not be much taper to indicate this, there is a practice, to help the muddle-headed, of trimming each root with a horizontal cross-cut at the top end but with a sloping cut at its base. These roots are tied in a bundle, with all the top ends level, and plunged upright into gravelly soil, with a couple of inches of this above the bundle. There they'll remain through the winter.

When young shoots are seen to be pushing through, in spring, the bundle is lifted, and the thongs separated and lined out 15in apart to grow on during the summer. In my experience, it is at this lining-out stage that great losses are easily incurred. It is so important not to allow the cuttings to dry out between lifting and replanting, when they'll be watered in. But you'll see a gardener with his line and a shallow trench drawn out alongside it, laying all the cuttings out at the correct spacing before he starts planting. The sun is shining, the wind blowing, but never mind; the cuttings are stiff and look unconcerned. In fact, they are being rapidly killed, so beware. And it isn't just seakale that suffers. There are many similar opportunities for killing, or maiming, plants at the lining-out stage. Until the last moment, always keep your planting-out material under moist wraps or in a plastic bag slightly moistened inside.

There are two ways of cropping seakale: either as perennials, located for a number of years in a selected spot (always in full sunshine and with maximum exposure); or for a single crop, after which the forced plants are discarded.

In the first case, plants are usually set out in a triangle or square with a spacing, ideally 15in, that will allow for covering them in winter, to provide total darkness. Even a crack of light will result in green shoots, which are bitter. They must be white. In the old days, the wild plants were blanched *in situ*, by piling mounds of shingle over their heads. But one who was at the receiving end of seakale forced in this way told me that the grit left in the shoots made chewing them a painful experience. (Bits of shell left in carelessly dressed crab cause similar explosions in the head.)

RIGHT, ABOVE *Seakale coming into flower*
RIGHT, BELOW *A mature seakale leaf*

There are purpose-made earthenware seakale pots which look most decorative standing around in the garden, and there are a few potters making them. They look like large, bulbous, upturned flower pots and are each fitted with a lid to place over the hole at the top. After the seakale thus blanched has been cut, the pots must be set aside and the plants allowed to grow naturally through the summer.

I prefer the second method, because it doesn't tie up any one piece of ground, where perennial weeds will be liable to creep in. Also it allows of heavier cropping. Every year you start afresh with a new lot of thongs, these being made from the previous season's crop when it is lifted in autumn. At that lifting, the core of the plant, with its terminal shoot bud or buds, is trimmed at the base to a length of 5 or 6in and these stout antlers are potted or boxed up in old potting soil, the shoot buds just at the surface when the container is full. They are then forced – in series, if you have enough filled containers – in darkness, at a temperature of 50°F/10°C, more or less. Under the stairs is often an excellent spot for this, or in a cellar, or even under the potting shed bench. There'll be no heat for forcing there, but you'll get your seakale in April, just the same.

The first shoots that are cut will be the best, because they will include the ultra-succulent flowering shoot (sometimes it really does taste of asparagus). If you have dachshunds, make sure they don't get at this before you. Likewise in the garden, before your plants can flower. They adore young flowering shoots.

You can go on cutting as further, thinner, shoots are made. No harm in weakening the roots, as they'll soon be thrown out, anyway. And next season's plants will already be lined out in the garden.

COOKING SEAKALE

Seakale needs only 15 minutes or so of boiling to make it tender and can then most simply be served with melted butter and a squirt of lemon juice. Or it can be coated with a sauce and/or sprinkled with a little Parmesan or Gruyère cheese and passed under the broiler. Like that, it deserves to be a course on its own.

Jane Grigson suggests covering it with a tomato *Sauce Aurore*, but I have yet to try this.

Cauliflower, Broccoli and Kale

*T*here has been and continues to be a considerable and confusing interchange of names among the brassicas that produce flowerets. Cauliflower nowadays includes all white types making one big, solid head. Those that overwinter and do not mature till spring used to be referred to as broccoli. That is no longer the case. The name broccoli is now applied to types which make numerous small shoots, though they may initially form a fair-sized central unit.

Calabrese is a particular form of broccoli, green and, in modern varieties, of quite a fair size on first maturing. This is popular in supermarkets and the breeders have aimed at a plant which can be harvested *in toto*, as soon as the central head has developed. In our gardens, however, we are interested in a long season with a succession of shoots, even though fairly small. So we retain our plants after the central head has been cut and may, in favourable circumstances, be able to continue cutting for a number of months. After one mild winter, I was still cutting at winter's end, having started in August.

There are many different kinds of sprouting broccoli in various colours, including white. 'Romanesco' is green, tinged purple, and should make a solid head coming to a peak in the centre. Having cut this head, there is little more to expect of the plant. But the strain has degenerated since it was first put out and often behaves like a sprouting broccoli, though maturing in October and November from a May sowing.

Purple-sprouting broccoli is sown in April and May and takes a year to

Purple-sprouting broccoli will produce a succession of heads (of decreasing size), if you keep up with cutting them as they develop

mature. It is divided, in the seed lists, into Early and Late. I grow both but can not honestly see any difference in maturing times between strains, though there are considerable differences between plant and plant. As purple-sprouting seldom reaches the markets and is not used commercially for canning or freezing, the breeders have done no work on it for many years.

Kale, or borecale, is extremely hardy and is ready to eat when young shoots are being made in spring. I should avoid the curly-leaved types. Pretty though they are, they are hard to clean and tend to be tough. There used to be a variety called 'Hungry Gap', which was so named, I always thought, because you had to have a very large and hungry gap in your stomach before you could face eating it.

But smooth-leaved cottagers' kale is another matter, and I always grow that, or the variant called 'Thousandhead'. Don't touch the plant till you see young side-shoots being made in early spring. These will be tender. Having picked them over, more shoots will develop, showing flower buds, but none the worse for that. The plants should be picked over every three days, in mild weather. That is where a deep-freeze comes in, as also for purple-sprouting. The really serious gap in one's own vegetable production tends to come in late May and most of June. These sprouting brassicas are a boon at that time (as are sprouting Brussels sprouts, if you have the space to leave them in the ground till early May).

Cultivating Brassicas

All the above require similar cultivation (though different timings) and are subject to similar pests and diseases. Rotations of where you grow them are important if club root (a self-descriptive disease) is to be avoided. Brassicas should never be grown on the same site two years running. Infected ground should be limed generously and rested from all cruciferous plants, including wallflowers and stocks (weeds like shepherd's purse and swine-cress can also be infected), for three years.

The position of your brassica seed bed should also be shifted annually. This is where you will direct-sow, in short rows, all those brassicas (and we also

RIGHT *Kale 'Thousandhead'*
PAGE 170 *The central rosette of a Brussels sprout*
PAGE 171 *A shoot of purple-sprouting broccoli*

include wallflowers), which will provide seedlings to be lined out – in June, most often – in their cropping positions. (The wallflowers will be shifted a second time, in autumn, to their spring bedding positions.)

It has to be added, however, that we are being more and more dragooned, through restricted choice, into growing F₁ hybrids, which are more profitable to the breeders. There are few seeds to a packet, and it is worth avoiding waste by sowing in a pot, and potting off the seedlings, individually, thereafter, before lining them out. Depredations by cabbage root fly are a danger at this stage. Their larvae hatch from eggs laid at the collar of the seedling, just above the soil surface, and they eat right through the stem. Commercial insecticides prescribe treatment.

We generally sow our brassica seed bed early, in late April, but some time in May is better for 'Romanesco'. The plants should be lined out in ground that was generously spread with bulky organic manure and then deeply dug the previous autumn or winter. A spacing of 30in between rows and 24in between plants will be right for most of them.

Cauliflowers are abundant and cheap in the shops in spring, and I don't grow them for harvesting then, nor those that mature in summer from a spring sowing. If they receive a check to their growth, as from drought or cold, they are apt to make tiny heads prematurely, and that's that. Besides, I have a kind of inbuilt resistance to eating brassicas when there is a tide of peas and beans coming in.

When I do like to cut cauliflowers is in autumn: October and November, even into December, if the weather is kind. Generally, they don't all mature at the same time but give you a good spread. There is a danger of frost spoiling the curds; so you should bend over some of the plant's longer leaves, to cover its vulnerable centre. The variety I have been growing of recent years is 'Barrier Reef', but that could change. Here is a case where anything described as 'new' in the seed lists is likely to have the advantage of not having had time to deteriorate since its recent distribution from the breeder. 'Romanesco' develops at about the same time.

Calabrese are mostly, perhaps all, F₁ hybrids, these days. 'Comet' from a mid-spring sowing in a pot, will mature in June – almost too early, as the plant has scarcely had the chance to develop enough foliage to see it through to a longer season. Caterpillars are the main problem with calabrese in summer.

The first – central – head developing on a calabrese plant

172

They are, before cooking, the same colour as the edible head, but become pale, and only too visible, once reduced to cooked corpses. You can, and should, soak each picking in salted water before cooking, but even though this will kill the creatures, it won't necessarily dislodge them. There is nothing for it but a vigilant and conscientious examination of what has been picked, breaking up the flower-bud clusters so that nothing escapes your beady eye.

Of greater value, I think, are the calabrese that make larger plants before cropping, from August on. 'Late Corona' or 'Express Corona' are of this type and are the ones that will, if healthy and if the autumn is open, continue productive for a long while. At Dixter we usually have to spray them with insecticide, at some stage, if the Large White butterfly larvae (large, rather handsomely marked creatures in clusters, that gradually disperse over the plant, as they grow) put in an appearance, as is the case when we get an invasion of the butterflies from the Continent, during the summer.

Purple-sprouting broccoli and kale have to run the gauntlet of winter. Their main enemy in my garden is the wood pigeon, in early spring, when green stuff becomes particularly attractive to them. They walk in to their food, only hopping on to the plant at the last moment. If, between short pieces of stick or cane, you stretch string round the patch in which the crop is growing, at a height above the ground of 6in or less, they are foiled. Bottles, painted bright red and fixed upside down over the top of 4ft canes among the plants, will act as a deterrent for a few days, but no longer.

When purple-sprouting is nearing the end of its season, it will produce a mass of quite tiny heads, which take a while to pick but are perfectly good if you include only a very short piece of stem behind the flower buds. The stem toughens quickly and the usual 10 minutes' boiling won't begin to soften it.

Purple-sprouting broccoli, picked, washed and ready for cooking

IN THE KITCHEN

Broccoli, calabrese and kale, simply boiled for 10 minutes and then seasoned, make such a good accompaniment to red meat (in particular), that I cook them in no other way. Jane Grigson gives some marvellous old Mediterranean recipes in her *Vegetable Book*, in which the broccolis become the protagonists. I shall try them in due course!

Cauliflower is a beautiful vegetable, but not one of the most interesting for flavour. It has a powerful, sulphurous smell through the house, so plenty of good ventilation is needed after cooking. It has a nice consistency, if not over-cooked, and is a good vehicle for other flavours, especially cheese.

The stem requires much longer to soften than the flowerets. Make a horizontal, transverse cut across the stem; or, if it is very thick, make two cuts into it to form a cross, so that boiling water can reach its core. Stand the cauliflower upright in a large saucepan of just enough boiling water to submerge the stem, but no more. Cover the pan. If the cauliflower projects above the lid, use foil instead. In 10 or 12 minutes from boiling being resumed, the flowerets will have steamed and the stem have cooked. Drain the cauliflower well.

CAULIFLOWER QUICHE

A quiche this size will make a light lunch or supper dish for 3. Substitute margarine for the lard in the piecrust dough if there are vegetarian considerations.

1½ quantities piecrust dough (see page 12)
1 medium-sized onion, *or*
2 or 3 shallots, finely chopped
2 tablespoons butter
1 medium-sized firm white cauliflower
1 egg
1 egg yolk
⅔ cup light cream
Salt and pepper
1½ tablespoons *each* grated Gruyère and Parmesan cheeses, mixed together

Roll out the dough and use it to line a 8–9in quiche dish. Leave it to rest in the refrigerator or a cool place for 30 minutes.

Place a baking sheet in the oven and preheat to 180°C/350°F/gas mark 4. Pre-bake the quiche shell for 15 minutes.

Meantime, cook the onion or shallots in the butter and spread over the base of the quiche shell. Over this, place a layer of steamed cauliflower flowerets, detached from the stem after steaming for 4 to 5 minutes (they should retain a little firmness). Arrange so that the tips of the flowerets project only a very little above the rim of the pastry.

Beat together the egg, the egg yolk and the cream, and season. Pour this mixture over the flowerets. Distribute the cheeses evenly over the top. Return the quiche to the oven and bake for 40 minutes. Eat while still warm, with a green salad.

CAULIFLOWER AU GRATIN

Cauliflower done in the Polish style is good, but a bit of a fiddle. Having to keep some of it warm while you finish off the rest is less convenient than finishing everything off together in the oven. Jane Grigson's cauliflower gratin, from her *Vegetable Book*, is most satisfactory in that way. If you had a heavy lunch, it is the perfect supper dish – or vice versa.

1 large firm white cauliflower
4 tablespoons butter
Mornay sauce made with 1¼ cups cauliflower stock and 1¼ cups milk and light cream combined (see page 142)

Gratin topping
2 tablespoons breadcrumbs
1 tablespoon *each* grated Gruyère and Parmesan cheeses, mixed together
1 tablespoon melted butter

Cook the cauliflower (see page 175), taking care when draining it to reserve enough cooking liquid as stock for making the mornay sauce.

While the sauce is simmering down, break up the cauliflower into pieces and fry them lightly in the butter, stirring them about so that they are evenly coated, but not brown. Now mix in a few tablespoons of the sauce.

Pour a layer of sauce into a gratin dish, arrange the cauliflower on top and pour over the rest of the sauce.

For the gratin finish sprinkle the top with the breadcrumbs and grated Parmesan and Gruyère. Drip the melted butter as evenly as possible over the crumbs and cheese. Bake in a preheated oven at 190°C/375°F/gas mark 5 until the top is brown.

Cabbage

*T*here are many kinds of cabbage and for every season, but I grow only one, a Savoy, 'January King'. The other kinds are easily bought in their season (if they have one), and that includes red cabbage. A red cabbage will keep fresh in my cool larder (no room in the refrigerator), apart from the outer two leaves, for weeks on end. If you grow your own, they'll all come on together and they will not hold on the plant till you get around to eating them. At their peak they are beautiful, but still a waste of space.

You see spring cabbage (usually sown in August) on sale in April and May, which is when you need it. But in my garden it never matured sufficiently to make cutting seem less than infanticidal, until early July. By then, I'm not in the mood for cabbage. Neither am I for summer cabbage that has been sown

A young, developing Savoy cabbage 'January King'

in spring and will come in simultaneously with delicious seasonal crops like peas and beans.

But winter is another matter. Savoy cabbages are outstandingly hardy. They are coarse and their foliage is deeply wrinkled, but 'January King' much less so than most. It has a characteristic purplish colouring on the outer leaves. The hearts are on the small side and plants can be set out 15in apart. It is included in the brassica seed bed (see page 168) that we sow in a small plot, outside, in late April and early May. The young plants are lined out on their cropping site late in June.

The one and only serious disease of cabbages and other brassicas on our heavy soil is that causing club root (you can't help recognizing it). To avoid this, never grow brassicas on the same site two years running. Look to your drainage, make your winter digging deep, incorporating plenty of compost or other bulky organic manure, and lime generously. After a couple of years of this treatment, infected ground will be safe again.

HARVESTING

After cutting your cabbages in the depths of winter, it is worth leaving the stumps and outer leaves (if you can still spare the space, that is). Young shoots produced in April will provide excellent spring greens as, simultaneously, do Brussels sprouts. If you have a lot of sprouting vegetables, all at the same time – quite possibly they will include turnips, purple sprouting broccoli and cottagers' kale – it is well worth blanching them for a minute in boiling water, cooling them rapidly in cold water and then putting them into bags for freezing. They'll come in handy, late in May, when supplies from the garden are at their lowest ebb.

Assuming that you have slug-infested ground, there will almost certainly be several small black slugs snugly nestled in the narrow gap between the base of the outer leaves and the central stem. These will have to be dealt with in the kitchen.

IN THE KITCHEN

Boiled cabbage is very good, I think, provided your house is well ventilated and you can quickly get rid of the sulphurous smell produced on cooking. Prepare a cabbage by first cutting it into quarters; then chopping out the white, central stem (my dachshunds love to scrunch these wedges); finally by shredding the leaves finely. Since the leaves, while stiff and fresh, take up a lot of space, rather than drop them into boiling water, it is easier to pack them, with some salt, into the empty saucepan first, and then pour on boiling water straight from a kettle, so as to reach two-thirds way or more up the cabbage. Ten minutes of hard boiling should be enough, once it has started. When the cabbage has softened a little, it can be turned over in the pan.

Drain really thoroughly, pressing out the moisture; then stir in freshly ground pepper and butter.

PARTRIDGE AND CABBAGE

A succulent dish, the cabbage quite counteracting any tendency to dryness in the birds. Now that chestnuts are available packaged in a ready-to-use state, their addition to this recipe is simple – and tasty. This will serve 3.

3 partridges
8oz bacon, cut across into
short, narrow strips
4 tablespoons butter
2 dozen small onions or, even better,
shallots, peeled
⅔ cup dry white wine
1¼ cups chicken, beef or
game stock (see page 13)
1 Savoy cabbage
Some cooked, peeled
chestnuts (optional)

Brown the birds and bacon in the butter in a skillet. Transfer them to a flameproof casserole, the birds placed breast down. Brown the onions or shallots in the butter and add them to the pot. Last, pour the

wine and stock into the frying juices, boil them, scraping the bottom and sides of the pan, and pour over the birds. Cover the casserole and either simmer on top of the stove or cook in a preheated oven at 160°C/325°F/ gas mark 3 for half an hour.

Meantime, blanch the cabbage, whole, for 10 minutes in a saucepan of boiling water. Remove the almost-cooked birds from the casserole while you put in the (still rather firm) cabbage, which you can split open by making a cross right through it with a knife or cleaver and spreading the quarters outwards. Add the chestnuts, if used, at this point. Return the birds, breasts uppermost, on to the cabbage bed. Replace the lid and cook for another quarter hour or so, testing the birds to make sure they are cooked. Place them, the cabbage and the bacon on a hot dish. Skim off any easily removable fat from the juices and reduce them on the stovetop, boiling hard till they are concentrated. Pour over the birds and serve.

SALADS

Lettuce

Endive

Corn
Salad

Cress

Cucumber

Sorrel

Orach

Salsify

Purslane

Fennel

Tomato

Rocket

Radish

Flowers

Salad Plants

I pride myself on my crisp, green salads, with a simple vinaigrette dressing. I can happily eat a large salad, every day in every season. On the whole, the British, at least in public places, produce disgusting salads, embedded in thick, glutinous dressings.

I have not fared much better with salads on the Continent, where the lettuce is drowned in a wet, vinegary dressing. The Americans understand these things far better and I have enjoyed their roadside salad bars. The various ingredients are fresh and simply presented and you can choose for yourself from a range of dressings, which form their own group.

Most of my friends enjoy Dixter salads and some of them know the garden well enough to be able to help in their collecting. Two or three of them, however, eat them as a duty – just one helping. Even then, Brad Sweet (Canadian) wears the silent, pained expression of a Christian martyr or of a lamb for the slaughter. But they are the exceptions.

Collecting a salad from the garden inevitably takes a little time, as there are so many individual items that are nice to use and, curiously, their flavours do not cancel each other out. You can still appreciate them individually, but those that would seem domineering tasted on their own often lose this harshness in the company of others and with emollient olive oil. The one exception that I would make to this rule is land cress (sometimes called American, though it is actually European). This is a nice-looking plant with foliage not unlike watercress, though neater. It is hardy and, from a late summer sowing, will provide fresh leaves right through the winter. But it's horribly aggressive and remains so even in mixed company. Just my opinion.

What does one use for a salad bowl? Fresh lettuce, in particular, is bulky and you want room for turning the dressing into the salad without a large part of it skipping out on to the table – or floor, where the dogs are waiting. You really need various bowls of different sizes. For the largest, I use the old basin from a ewer and basin outfit that is normally in my bedroom (for ornament; we do have bathrooms and running water). Next size down, and still pretty capacious, is one of Alan Caiger-Smith's bowls from his Aldermaston factory,

PAGE 180 *A photogenic but badly grown lettuce*
PAGE 181 *Salsify bolting in spring; the raw buds are good in salads*

now closed, alas. His bold and lively brushwork and fresh colours – none of the murky greens and browns that are so fashionable on heavy pottery that no washing-up machine could ever weaken – are a constant joy.

I have a preference for china over wood, for this purpose; but some cooks like the fact that wood takes up flavours, especially garlic, which can simply be wiped over the surface, before the salad is added. Afterwards, another wipe with a paper towel is all the cleansing that's required. Or is it? I have uneasy doubts about this. Hence, china for me.

VINAIGRETTE DRESSING

I think I make a good dressing, but I rarely include garlic. It isn't that I dislike raw garlic (if I'm not being anti-social) but that its flavour is pervasive. I like it for a change, not as a routine. So, when Beth Chatto is staying, she often makes the dressing and always includes garlic and that is nice, *for a change!* When she has left, it is again nice to return to my normal routine.

The ingredients are normally in a cluster on the kitchen table (which is large and long). But since this is usually the coldest room in the house, the olive oils are apt to turn solid, which is a sign of pedigree, in a way, but they have to be reliquified in the neighbouring dining-room.

Into a bowl, I first grind some coriander seed (keeping a grinder for this alone). That needs to go in before the black pepper, so that I can see how much I've used. Its aroma is beguiling. Sea salt and black pepper follow; then Dijon mustard, followed by balsamic vinegar, to taste. I'm not heavy on this. My friend Colin Hamilton prefers lemon juice to vinegar. Much as I

love lemon, I do enjoy the flavour of vinegar for this purpose. I like the taste of a good vinegar. I don't include sugar.

Having mixed the ingredients up to this point, I am very generous with the final one, olive oil. Of this, I add two grades – one a fairly ordinary Italian oil that I buy wholesale in large tins; that's so as not to be too extravagant. But I am no less generous, often more so, with the best first-pressing olive oil that I can find. The flavour is so good that the fact of a bottle costing as much as a bottle of good wine can be discounted. The bottle of oil will last for quite a while; the wine will be gone at a sitting. One has to keep a sense of proportion. Often, I also include a *little* of the oil in which Italian sun-dried tomatoes are preserved.

All these ingredients are whisked together, vigorously, and immediately tipped over the salad. I find that I can get nearly all the dressing out of the basin with the rounded end of the salad serving spoon without resorting to a scraper.

Lettuce

Lettuce and endives are the mainstays to provide bulk for a crisp, green salad; endives from autumn to spring, lettuce in the other half of the year. Of course, with a little protection, lettuce can be grown year round. I can't be bothered with the protection. So, from November to May I rely on endives and on bought lettuce – 'Iceberg' (which keeps well in the refrigerator) and 'Little Gem' (which doesn't). Lettuces that have grown slowly in winter can be extremely bitter – 'Winter Density', for instance.

The great thing is to have no gaps between lettuce crops from June to October. What is liable to happen, if you employ a gardener to grow your vegetables for you, is that a huge crop comes along late in June. There's no hope of getting through it before it bolts. But there is no follow-up. For crisp, crunchy lettuces, a series of sowings is obligatory. Those made in spring yield the best results most easily. Later sowings run up against high temperatures, which inhibit germination, and water shortages.

If you are sowing in hot weather, lower the temperature by watering the drill before sowing and choose late afternoon for your sowing time, so that temperatures will be falling and the seeds' first experience of the wide world will be of damp and of cooling night temperatures. As to moisture, irrigation will be a great help but is not always possible. It is particularly important that the ground should have been deeply cultivated and generously laced with water-retentive organic goodies.

HEARTED LETTUCES

Of lettuces that make hearts, there are the long-leaved cos types (called romaine in the United States and France) and the globular cabbage lettuce, divided into crispheads and butterheads. On the whole, avoid the latter, which are flimsy and with little character or flavour. I do sometimes grow one, from Suttons, called 'Suzan' because it matures quickly from a late July sowing. That is a late sowing date for successfully maturing lettuce as an outdoor crop, before the arrival of bad weather.

'Iceberg' and 'Webb's Wonderful' are crispheads and I honestly think it's best to buy them. 'Iceberg' is on sale throughout the year. When I grow them myself, I find that I cannot cope with much of the mature crop before it rots

– from the centre outwards.

'Little Gem', which is a rather stumpy cos, is my, and everyone else's, favourite; at once sweet (it used to be called 'Sugar Cos') and bitter and with a wonderful crunch when well-grown, and having a dense heart. Early July is as late as we can sow this, and even then success is generally partial, although we have been pretty successful since Perry Rodriguez took over.

My first sowing, however, is in March, in a pot in a cold frame. Sowing lettuce seed is always satisfying, as it is almost white and so you can see exactly where it has

'Little Gem', best of all lettuces

dropped on to darker soil or compost. The seedlings are pricked out, 7 by 4, into a couple of seed trays, hardened off and planted out before the seedlings are large enough to spoil one another. Beware, at this stage, of depredations by pigeons or other hungry competitors.

A few weeks after this sowing, we make another, again of 'Little Gem', direct into the open ground. The seedlings should make quite large plants, even though their habit is compact, so thinning can be to 8 or 9in.

LOOSE-LEAF LETTUCES

Loose-leaf, or loosehead, lettuces make no hearts. You can either pick leaves from them, piecemeal, or cut an entire rosette of leaves, leaving the stem to sprout again. The bright green 'Salad Bowl' is the best-known variety and it has wavy-margined foliage but little texture.

'Red Salad Bowl' and other 'red' (greenish-brown, actually) loose-leafs are very pretty, growing, but rather pathetic once you get them indoors, especially after being dressed, when their lack of texture appears doubly limp. Probably they are best as ornaments for the formal *potager*. 'Salad Bowl' has advantages. If you're not in a hurry to pick it, it just keeps on growing, till the

185

rosette of young foliage stands perhaps 12in high where it is much less prone to slug damage. Bolting occurs only late in the autumn.

Towards the end of May, I like to make a direct sowing of mixed lettuce varieties. They will mature at different rates, which is useful, and some will hold longer than others. They'll include cos, cabbage and loose-leaf types. Thompson & Morgan's 'Fresh Salad Mixed' is such a mixture.

IN THE KITCHEN

Large pieces of lettuce leaf are awkward to handle in a salad. I don't like tearing them, myself. The result looks disagreeable. Shredding should be out of the question. So I take the tip of a stainless steel knife and cut the leaf (or several leaves one on top of the other) two or three times, longitudinally, then two or three times transversely. They remain fair-sized pieces, but easily managed.

LETTUCE SOUP

When lettuces bolt, or sprout again from the original cut, you can still make use of the greenery. From *Jane Grigson's Vegetable Book* comes a soup. See also *Duck Stewed with Green Peas*, page 152.

2 tablespoons butter
1 large onion, chopped
1 clove garlic, chopped
About 8oz lettuce leaves and stem, sliced
1 tablespoon all-purpose flour
4½ cups light chicken stock (see page 13; water it down, if necessary), heated
Salt, pepper
⅔ cup heavy or whipping cream
1 extra-large egg yolk
Chopped fresh parsley or, preferably, chervil
Croûtons of bread fried in butter

Melt the butter in a pan and cook the onion and garlic slowly for 5 minutes, then stir in the lettuce. Mix everything around for a minute or two, then sprinkle on the flour. Stir again and cook for a minute, then gradually add the hot stock. Simmer for 5 minutes (or longer if you include tough lettuce stem). Purée the soup in a blender or food processor; pour it into the rinsed-out pan through a sieve. If puréeing has made the soup too thick, dilute it with water. Correct the seasoning.

Bring the soup to boiling point. Whisk the cream and egg yolk together. Pour on a ladle of boiling soup and whisk again. Return to the pan and rewarm for a minute but don't allow the soup to boil. Stir in chopped parsley or chervil. Serve with the croûtons.

Endive

*E*very lover of green salads has taken the endives on board long since. But all endives have, to quote Joy Larkcom in *The Salad Garden,* 'a very characteristic flavour, with a slightly bitter edge to it. It's addictive to those who acquire the taste, but less popular with the sweet-toothed.' However, as she goes on to explain, the bitterness can easily be modified by including blander salad ingredients, by your choice of variety and by the time of year or the age or part of the plant that you eat. Even the bitter roots must have a certain attraction, because my dachshunds salvage them from where old roots have been discarded, carry them triumphantly into the garden and, after a few bites, leave them on a lawn, looking like dead rats. Endive is certainly addictive to them.

Endive is a native perennial of Europe with very thick tap roots. You see it flowering along roadsides, especially near the sea. Its pure blue flowers are beautiful individually, but never borne in sufficient abundance to conceal the scrawniness of the plant bearing them. Each bloom lasts for no more than a few morning hours.

In Britain, till quite recently, when colourful endives first appeared in supermarkets, most people's idea of endives was an almost white, bullet-shaped object, obviously forced in the dark and crunchy to bite. That crunchiness is one of the most engaging characteristics of what is known as Belgian endive. This variety originated and was developed in the 1840s in Belgium, where it remains a major industry. There are also the red-leaved kinds, or red and white or some other attractive variegation, which have been developed in Italy. And there are green endives. We can grow them all, though some are hardier than others.

Belgian endive was the first kind that I grew; it is expensive to buy. We sow the seed in May. If the seed is an F_1 hybrid, I recommend buying two packets, to allow for fewer seeds and the necessary thinning of seedlings. Unfortunately, not many firms are offering Belgian endive seed of any kind, at the time of writing.

Sow in a shallow drill and thin the seedlings to 9in apart if you want really fat chicons which, of course, we all do. Leave the plants to grow till late autumn and lift them before any severe frost has damaged or killed the exposed top of the root. Twist off any old leaf remains.

At this stage, more than one course is open to you, depending on the facilities you have for growing the roots in dark places. At Dixter, we put into winter use the very large pots that have been standing on our terrace, filled with tender ornamentals. The roots are shortened at the base so as to be up to 10in long (this depends on the depth of your containers – a wooden box might be less deep). The roots are stood upright on a couple of inches of soil, and packed very close one to another, but with just enough space between to make it possible to work in old potting compost, right up to their necks, but leaving the crowns uncovered.

We used to cover the crowns, making a sleeve of polythene to contain the peat or sand topping. A weight on the crowns has the advantage of keeping the chicons closed when they push up. However, for one reason and another, we have discontinued the covering. Sand, or grit, is well draining, so that no rotting ensues; but it is difficult to wash every grain of it away before eating the endive. Peat is better, if it doesn't get wet, when it encourages rot to set in. Now we have dispensed with the covering, we give a heavy watering just before bringing the pots inside and that lasts for a number of weeks. When further watering becomes necessary, I make sure that no water lodges in the plant crowns.

One pot is stood on the billiard room stairs, which is our warmest dark spot (but there is desperate destruction if the dogs can get at it). Another goes into a cool cellar and any more stand in a shed, covered with several layers of burlap. So they develop in rotation and keep me in endive from early in the year until early May.

If you haven't many dark places for your roots, lay most of them in damp sand in a pretty cold spot and cover them. Subsequently, pack them upright, as described, into some container in a warmer spot, but this must be dark. If it is handy for the kitchen, that helps. You won't welcome too much scurrying around for salad ingredients. There are certain varieties of red-leaved endive which 'heart up' and can be treated in the same way.

Now for the kinds that are grown in daylight throughout. Thompson & Morgan's 'Saladisi' mixture includes several leaf endives, some green, some red, some stripy. The mixture is sown in late June or early July and I allow the endives to grow untouched for the rest of the season, while I make use of quick developers. Thompson & Morgan keep changing the composition of the

Belgian endive being kept dark till ready for use

Green endive from 'Saladisi' mixture

mixture, yet without stating what it includes; so I am liable to find that an ingredient on which I was relying has vanished without warning or explanation. The quick developers may include purslane, several lettuces, chervil, arugula, scallion, basil – the last two hopelessly squashed out by their more vigorous neighbours. That is the trouble with mixtures. It is definitely better, if the time and space can be found, to sow each salading in part of a row on its own. But I still sow 'Saladisi' for convenience. The endives come into their own in late autumn and then, again, quite early in the New Year; certainly by February. And I can go on cutting as late as May. The colour in the coloured endives is brightest while the weather is still cold and their appearance certainly enlivens my salads.

The green-leaved 'Sugar Loaf' endive is the third kind that I grow. A row of this is sown in well-nourished ground at the turn of June–July. If the weather is hot and dry, germination will be erratic. Water the bottom of the drill that you have drawn out, before sowing.

The plants should grow large and on thinning be allowed a 12in spacing in the row. By October, they will have hearted up – into a cumbersome apparatus, slightly resembling cos lettuce but much heavier. Slugs go for them in a big way, but you can discard many outer leaves, which are more bitter and less succulent than those towards the centre. This part of the endive will keep perfectly fresh for a week, stored in a polythene bag in the refrigerator. Along with lettuce, it should form one of the bulk ingredients in your green salads.

'Sugar Loaf' endive hearting up

The 'Sugar Loaf' plants are fairly susceptible to frost, but even when the outer layers have become limp and transparent, the centre will often remain unaffected. Always cut your 'Sugar Loaf' very low while still leaving a stump, which will sprout again in the spring, so that the young shoots can be included in salads once more. By January, my wretched dachshunds have eaten out all remaining hearts, even if the weather has been mild up to then.

IN THE KITCHEN

If you grow your Belgian endive well and have plenty of it, cooking it will not seem too extravagant. Here is Jane Grigson's *Endive with Cream*, which can be served as a vegetable with a roast bird or joint of meat. Instead of cream, the concentrated meat juices may be substituted.

191

ENDIVE WITH CREAM

Allow one or two Belgian endive heads per person. Trim and boil for about 10 minutes in a large pan, so that when well drained the chicons lie in a single layer. Melt a large knob of butter and turn the endives in this, at a low heat, until it begins to turn golden.

Finally pour in some cream – a table-spoon per head of endive – raise the heat and bubble the whole thing so that the liquids combine into a small amount of rich savoury sauce. Keep turning the endives. The outer part should be meltingly succulent, contrasting with the inner core that still retains a certain bite.

ENDIVE WITH HAM AND CHEESE SAUCE

This is another good Grigson method and an irresistible combination, as she rightly claims. I prefer to cook a joint of ham on the bone, as it is so much tastier than any-thing you can buy ready-cooked (see page 147). Serves 3 to 6 as a supper or light lunch dish, 6 as a starter.

6 fat heads of Belgian endive, trimmed
Salt (optional)
Lemon juice
Sugar
6 thin slices of ham
Dijon mustard
Butter
2½ cups mornay sauce, preferably made with stock from boiling the ham (see page 142)
Extra Parmesan cheese
Any breadcrumbs

Blanch the endive for 10 minutes in boil-ing, salted water (omit salt if the stock is salty), with a squeeze of lemon juice and a pinch of sugar. Drain thoroughly. Spread each slice of ham with a little mustard and wrap it around a head of endive.

Butter a gratin dish and fit in the swaddled endive, flap sides down so that it stays neat. Pour over the sauce and scatter with cheese and breadcrumbs. Bake for about 20 minutes in the oven preheated to 190–220°C/375–425°F/gas mark 5–7. Remove when it looks as good as it smells, with a golden-brown top.

Corn Salad

This is a far more popular salading in France, where it is called *mâche*, than in England, although it is remarkably hardy and is, indeed, a native of arable land, sand dunes and other dry spots where there is not too much competition. It has a wide distribution through Europe and beyond. It is an annual, but once established in your garden, it will self-sow and keep going, in paving cracks, for instance. But richer fare is needed to produce a

Corn salad, also known as mâche *or lamb's lettuce*

worthwhile leaf crop, for the spathulate leaves are small at the best of times. A member of the valerian family, *Valerianella locusta* is its botanical name; lamb's lettuce is another English name for it.

It is February as I write, and I have had several goes at the corn salad 'Cavallo', from Thompson & Morgan, that we sowed at the end of last August. But it needs quite a long growing season and, the seed being hard, does not germinate readily in dry weather unless the drill in which you sow is well watered beforehand. Thin to 6in apart. The protection of cloches will produce an earlier and lusher crop, but I don't bother.

At Dixter we make the one sowing, but you can obtain an autumn crop from a summer sowing and a spring crop from an early spring sowing, although you then run into the plant's urge to flower rather than to make leaves. The tiny flowers are a very pale blue, easily recognized once identified. The whole plant is no more than a few inches high. It would generally be tedious to pick leaves individually. Better to slash a number of them at a time with a knife.

IN SALADS

The flavour is mild, but distinct and very pleasing. It is a good thing, in a mixed salad, to include plenty of mild flavours to balance those that are strong – particularly strong at winter's end, when growth has been slow, which concentrates flavour. Such are chervil, mizuna and pak choi.

193

Cress

Cress is an ill-defined word. The kind of 'cress' that is scattered over your pub sandwich is generally salad rape, *Brassica napus*. This has a milder flavour than white mustard, *Sinapis alba*, which may also masquerade as cress. Such 'cress' is grown for its seed leaves (cotyledons), which are rounded, not linear, as are the true garden cress's, *Lepidium sativum*. Garden cress seed takes nearly twice as long to grow, ready for cutting, as that of mustard or salad rape, so these last are preferred in the trade, but so is the word cress.

I get a packet of garden cress seed, each year, and make one sowing, in late February or early March, using the entire packet (which has a lot of seed in it), on one seed tray. Never cover the seed; it should lie on the surface of whatever compost you are using, otherwise some of this will be carried up on the foliage, and washing is made more difficult. The brown seed coats will sometimes be carried upwards on the leaf, but are not important.

I germinate the seed in a cold frame, kept close. The seed must never be allowed to dry out. After the first two or three days, there should be plenty of light available so that you get bright green, stocky seedlings. When the seedlings are a couple of inches high, or slightly less, I water the tray heavily from below, let it drain and then bring it into the kitchen, where it sits on a window sill. There I cut from it as necessary, with a sharp knife.

Garden cress can form an ingredient in a green salad and its sharp, individual, but by no means overwhelming, flavour is one of the best for making cress sandwiches. So many saladings are available after March that I don't bother with any more cress, but it can be grown for its true leaves, in which case the seedlings are given much more space, and the plants will be of the cut-and-come-again type.

Another excellent salad ingredient over a long period was called 'Mega Cress' by Thompson & Morgan, though it goes by other names elsewhere, which is annoying (especially as Thompson & Morgan have currently given up listing it). I try to save my own seed but it is not always convenient to keep old plants for this purpose. It is a broad-leaved cress and is sometimes listed as such. In summer, it runs to flower and seed much too quickly, so the best

The broad-leaved 'Mega Cress'

time to sow (which also avoids depredations by flea beetle) is in early autumn, outside. You wait for the true leaves to develop; these are paddle-shaped with a somewhat frilly margin. From October on, you'll be including this in every salad until very severe weather may finish the plants off, but they often last the winter through. The spicy flavour is individual and quite strong, but not noticeably so once in the company of lettuce or Belgian endive.

If you can allow your plants to self-sow, germination will be over a period, which is an advantage, giving you a succession of lusty young seedlings.

There is an annual weed, widespread in gardens and an extremely prolific self-seeder, called hairy bitter cress (*Cardamine hirsuta*). It isn't noticeably hairy. The leaves are pinnate, with rounded segments and they are collected into rosettes. These are hardly noticeable in summer, when it is so busy reproducing that it hasn't the time for much foliage. But on well-nourished soil, quite large, almost non-flowering plants will develop, being at their leafiest in early spring. It is well worth cutting the foliage, then, to include in salads. Pigeons may join you, as they are fond of the young shoots when they begin to run up to flower.

The ripe seeds, incidentally, are ejected from May on, with considerable force. If you like to do your weeding on a kneeling mat, with your eyes close to what you're doing, the seeds will jump into your eyes. An old Scottish cousin of mine, Mary Finlay, used to call it 'Jumping Jesus'. And she was a pious lady.

WATERCRESS

Most of us do not have the right conditions – a pure, flowing stream – for the ideal cultivation of watercress. I certainly haven't. But it can be grown without such facilities if damp shade can be provided. Joy Larkcom (in *The Salad Garden*) suggests buying a packet of fresh watercress from a supermarket, pinching out the tips of the shoots and then standing the leafy stems in water, in a light place, where they will quickly root (or rot, in my editor's case).

Later, they can be planted out, but this transition needs to be carefully managed. Pot up your rooted cuttings individually, and keep them under protected glass until established in compost. Then harden the plants off, eventually planting them out in that damp, partially shaded spot which I hope you have.

I have grown watercress from seed and have once grown it to an edible condition with partial success. That's not much to boast of. In its second year, my small colony flowered incontinently and seemed to lose interest in producing leaves.

Some people use land cress (see page 182) as an alternative to watercress; but I find the taste too aggressive.

Cucumber

Most of the marrow and cucumber family, Cucurbitaceae, produce watery or pulpy fruits which are scarcely worth eating. Few of their advocates like to admit this, because they are beautiful and they are fun. I always grow some ornamental gourds, but when asked whether they are edible, am somewhat nonplussed for a reply. Edible doesn't necessarily correlate with nice to eat.

There are zucchini, of course; but unless you gather them daily, they in no time enlarge into the marrows which they really are. I don't like being hounded by my vegetables – snow peas and sugar snap peas are similarly demanding. Sometimes it's nice not to have to think about them daily. Life is already complicated with dogs and cats, not to mention humans.

Cucumbers, whose flavour is so fresh and whose crunch is so amorous, are in a class of their own. Only too often, we fail with them at Dixter through some inattention in the early stages, and I do so miss having my own. Bought cucumbers, even when they come small, in neat packages, are never the same thing. Why so? Chiefly because the skins of travelling cucumbers are deliberately bred to be tough, and I think the skin should be eaten. The flesh itself is much more chewy and indigestible in the market-produced article. You should, unless burdened with a sad, individual weakness, be able to eat raw cucumber without a thought of subsequent discomfort.

Ridge cucumber was (and still sometimes is) the description given to the kind that can be grown unprotected, once past the seedling stage. It makes shortish, zeppelin-shaped fruits. Except for a slightly spiny exterior, easily rubbed off, it can be as good to eat as anything you meet today. But now and again it used to turn up a plant whose every fruit was incorrigibly bitter. In modern seed strains that rarely happens, although I should add that the stem end of any cucumber is quite often bitter and should automatically be rejected.

Fashions affect cucumbers, and tiny-fruited varieties seem to be in. It is not so easy to find the long, narrow kinds, which I favour (you may want to cut them into boat-shaped pieces), but they are about. There is also a fashion for seedless, unpollinated cucumbers. This is nonsense. Cucumbers are never more than half-grown when gathered and the seeds are perfectly soft and edible. They are, moreover, beautifully arranged, which can be appreciated when the fruit is sliced transversely.

We never try and rush things at Dixter, and I find that an early May sowing in a snug cold frame is quite soon enough. Seeds of modern F_1 hybrids are horribly expensive (that's the main point about them, for the seed merchants), I used to sow two seeds to a pot, later discarding one of them if both germinated. But if the packet contains only five seeds, you are more careful and sow singly, discarding the pot if nothing appears in it! If there are as many as twelve seeds in a packet, save half of them for next year; they keep all right. If sowing in plastic pots, remember that overwatering before germination is only too easy, but will rot the seeds.

By the time the seedlings have been hardened off, it will be mid-June and that is early enough to be planting out. Organic-rich soil in a sunny position sheltered from wind is what you should be looking for. In some ways, a compost heap is ideal and is what we use, the heap having originated from grass mowings off our meadow areas. But don't make cucumbers share their bed with gourds or marrows. They will get swamped.

If the cucumbers are lying against a heap of soil, they will be pale on the underside. That doesn't really matter. Slugs may damage their skins; you can do something about that. Third possible snag: long, typically shaped cucumbers won't ever be straight. They'll be curved. If you're not selling them, that's no worry, either. Still, if it's not inconvenient to have them clambering up some support, like netting, the cucumbers will hang free and will be straight, which looks nice.

Once they get going, growth is amazingly rapid, and you'll be picking before the end of July. Regular picking will enable the plants to prolong their cropping, but pick while the fruits are still relatively small.

A handy cucumber just right for use

IN THE KITCHEN

Wrapped in polythene, cucumbers keep fresh in the refrigerator for several days. Nearly everyone loves cucumber sandwiches, especially if well buttered and if both bread and cucumber are thinly cut. You'll have to learn to cut your own bread from a loaf (sliced bread as bought is never thin enough); the texture must not be too open. You may or may not wish to peel the cucumber but it will be the better for a bit of softening. Salt the slices an hour before use and pour off the juice thereby released. Don't let this moisture extraction go on for too long or there'll be no bite left in the cucumber.

CUCUMBER SOUP

This is my own, straightforward recipe. The first recipe that I used for making it was quite unnecessarily laborious. Furthermore, after instructing you to remove the skin, it recommended the use of artificial green colouring, in order to restore the colour that had been removed. Admittedly, tough-skinned cucumbers are what you normally buy, but those of your own raising should be thin-skinned. Even though flecks of skin will still be visible after blending, I should include at least half, if not all of it.

1 large cucumber, or equivalent in
smaller ones, diced
1 onion, chopped
4 tablespoons butter
6½ cups chicken or other light stock, hot
(see page 13; dilute if necessary)
Salt and pepper
2 egg yolks

2 tablespoons heavy cream
Extra knob of butter
Chopped parsley
Croûtons of bread fried in butter (optional)

Sweat the onion slowly in the butter, in a covered pan, for 5 minutes. Add the cucumber and sweat for another 5 minutes. Add rather more than half the preheated stock. Simmer till the cucumber is cooked – about 15 minutes. Blend in an electric blender or food processor, adding the rest of the stock so as to obtain a thinnish liquid. Season. Reheat in the same pan and pour a ladleful into a basin in which egg yolks and cream have been beaten together. Return this to the pan and warm through – but don't boil – for just long enough to thicken the soup. Add the knob of fresh butter and stir in the parsley. It is nice served with croûtons of bread.

RUSSIAN CUCUMBER AND SORREL SOUP

This is from *Jane Grigson's Vegetable Book*. In a footnote, she says that spinach can be used instead of sorrel but recommends an increase of lemon juice, to achieve the right degree of sharpness. (I have success-fully substituted bolting lettuces, which have quite a bitter element in them.) To gain the strong cucumber flavour that I like, I use twice as much as she gives, 1lb instead of ½lb. The eggs should be boiled for no more than 8 minutes.

8oz sorrel
Generous ¾ cup heavy and light cream mixed
1¼ cups plain yogurt
2¼ cups beef stock or beef consommé, chilled
5 cups chopped cucumber
3 hard-boiled eggs, chopped

Chopped fresh chives
Chopped green fennel or tarragon
Salt and pepper
Lemon juice

Remove the thickest sorrel stems (but if picking it yourself, you will only take the blades anyway), rinse and cut up roughly. Put into a pan with no extra water and stir over a moderate heat until reduced to a dark green purée. Put into a big soup tureen and leave to cool. Add the remaining ingredients in the order given, mixing them in well and adjusting the quantities of herbs and seasonings to taste. Serve well chilled.

To enjoy this, some of my young friends seem to need a bit of training. They are unused to the idea of cold soups.

CACIK

Fergus Garrett, my head gardener and great friend, is half-Turkish. He gave me this as a Turkish recipe, pronounced 'judjik', though it is widespread in the Middle East, as a classic cucumber and yogurt salad. It is also quoted by Jane Grigson who recom-mends serving it with whole-wheat bread. She mentions, too, that it can be diluted with extra yogurt and served as a soup. I make it as a salad side-dish to accompany lamb.

1 large cucumber or its equivalent in smaller ones
Sea salt, finely ground
3–5 cloves garlic

2¼ cups plain yogurt
1 tablespoon chopped dill or 4 tablespoons of chopped fresh mint
Olive oil
Cayenne pepper

Dice the cucumber, preferably unpeeled. Put in a colander sprinkled with finely ground sea salt. Leave for 1 hour, then squeeze out the juice. Meantime, peel the cloves of garlic and pound them to a pulp with a little sea salt (to taste) in a mortar. Mix this pulp into the yogurt, then mix in the cucumber and dill or mint. Chill. Turn into a dish, pour over a little olive oil and a sprinkling of the red pepper.

Sorrel

The sharp, fresh flavour of sorrel is akin to lemon. Undiluted, it can be a little disturbing, but combined with other flavours it is a great ingredient. We never grew it when I was young and it was only when I began to take the preparation of the food at home entirely into my own hands that sorrel entered my life. I suspect this to be the case with many another of my coutry-men. An increased awareness of continental – especially French – cookery has enriched our lives.

There are two principal species of sorrel. *Rumex acetosa* is a British native and abundant in our meadow areas. Some 2ft tall at flowering, it contributes a delightful haze of warm red. However, the leaves, albeit of good flavour, are too fibrous of texture, even at their youngest, in spring.

The species on which to concentrate is the south European *R. scutatus,* which, as the name describes, has (inverted) shield-shaped leaf blades. The texture is soft, almost fleshy, and entirely devoid of fibre.

The easiest way to raise stock is from seed, sown in a pot, the seedlings, when large enough to handle, lined out where they will remain. I recommend an open position. Sorrel doesn't mind shade but mine, under a pear tree, becomes sullied by bird droppings from the branches above. If you are gathering clean, fresh salading from the garden, you may not want to wash and get it wet, so clean sorrel foliage is a help.

From a batch of seedlings, you will notice that some produce a greater abundance of sizeable and usable leaves than others, or are less hell-bent on running up to flower. You can mark such plants and use them when the

The shield-shaped leaves of sorrel, Rumex scutatus

time comes for remaking your patch – say once in three years. Division of stock in autumn or spring is the simplest operation.

One of the useful sorrel attributes is its extended season. You can pick plenty of leaves from March to November and a few even through winter. In May, the plants have a great urge to flower and nothing will stop them, but you must cut down the flowering stems to encourage further foliage production; also to forestall self-seeding, which could be a nuisance. From midsummer on, the plants will behave more amenably.

IN THE KITCHEN

Fresh in a salad, you need only a few leaves, cut up. Similarly with spinach, whose flavour is almost as sharp. There are also good sorrel sauce recipes to go with fish, two of them quoted by Jane Grigson in her *Fish Cookery*.

GREEN SORREL SOUP

This is the most popular soup I make and I discovered it in *Jane Grigson's Vegetable Book*, where it appears as 'Margaret Costa's Green Soup'. It is because the leaves are fibreless that they need no cooking and this preserves their fresh green colouring. Serves 4.

2 good handfuls sorrel
3 tablespoons butter
½ onion, finely chopped
2 medium potatoes, peeled, diced (about 1½ cups)
4½ cups homemade chicken stock, heated (see page 13)
Salt, pepper, grated nutmeg, pinch of sugar
4 tablespoons heavy cream
Chopped fresh chives
Croûtons of bread fried in butter

Melt the butter and cook the onion in it till soft but not brown. Stir in the potatoes and stock. Add seasoning. Simmer until the potatoes are cooked. Meanwhile, cut away any thick stems from the sorrel and wash it well. If picking your own, simply break off the blades, leaving the stems behind.

Purée the soup in the blender or food processor with the sorrel leaves, until smooth and bright green. You will have to do this in batches. Return it to the pan, check the seasoning and consistency, adding more stock or water if necessary, and reheat without boiling (if you boil the soup, the sorrel will become dark green and lose the full vigour of its flavour). If the soup is on the thick side, dilute it with water or more stock.

Add the cream and chives, and serve with small cubes of bread fried golden-brown in butter.

This soup can also be served chilled, but it will need a little more cream and quite a lot more liquid.

Orach

Although related to spinach, orach (or orache), *Atriplex hortensis*, is better used in one of its brightly coloured leaf forms (generally reddish-purple) as an enlivener of green salads in early summer. The purple- and red-leaved kinds are beautiful plants and they self-sow like crazy. We have them in various borders and the seedlings need rigorous thinning. Starting from scratch, you can broadcast the seed. Green capsid bugs love to eat the young shoots. If you don't know what these insects look like, examine your orach plants, as the capsid's bright green colouring shows up particularly well against the colourful leaves.

Orach will grow 6ft tall. As it runs to seed, normally in August, the flattened seed capsules are as bright as the rest of the plant and are most ornamental. Good for picking but heavy if left on the plant, which may sway over unless supported with a cane and tie. By late summer, the seed is ripening and turning brown. It is wise to pull the plants out at this stage, so as not to be overwhelmed by self-sowns the next year.

The young leaves in salads are as colourful as flowers. Orach can be cooked as a spinach substitute but the flavour is unexciting and, anyway, there is seldom enough of it in soft condition to make a decent dish.

Salsify

This is a fleshy-rooted biennial closely related to scorzonera. I have grown them concurrently and decided that salsify is slightly better flavoured.

Salsify is grown both for its root, for winter eating and for its sprouting shoots in late spring salads. As it is a ground keeper, like parsnip, it should be sown and grown where the plants, which are hardy, will not get in your way at the end of their term.

The ground must not be recently manured, otherwise the roots will branch. It should have been deeply dug and manured for the previous crop. Sow in

Purple orach: the leaves and shoots are good both raw and cooked

Salsify growing between beets and chrysanthemums

1in-deep drills in April and thin the seedlings finally to be 10–12in apart. The roots can be lifted right through the winter.

In spring, the plants run up to 3ft or more to flower, which is when their side-shoots, each containing a flower bud, come in as a salad ingredient. The flowers are a rich shade of purple, opening in the morning but going to bed at noon.

IN THE KITCHEN

Scrub the roots; then scrape the skin off them with the edge of a knife. The white flesh thus exposed instantly discolours. There is nothing you can do about this but as soon as each root has been scraped, rinse it and then drop it into a saucepan with salted cold water and a little malt vinegar. Cook the roots whole, if not too long, boiling them for 20 minutes. Then pour off the water, cut the roots up transversely into rounds and finish them off at a low heat in butter. The flavour is enhanced at this stage by the addition of chopped parsley, the grated rind of half a lemon and a finely chopped clove of garlic. Salsify goes well served with chicken. Sometimes known as vegetable oysters; one can (just about) take the point.

As an ingredient in salads, trim back the long, whiskery outer bracts so that you are just using the flower buds whole.

206

Purslane

escribed in my *Flora* as a cosmopolitan weed of warm temperate and sub-tropical climates, purslane, *Portulaca oleracea*, certainly loathes a damp, chilly summer. It is an annual, about 6in tall, with rounded, fleshy leaves. It is that fleshiness that is so beguiling, as you scrunch. It seems that there is a golden-leaved form, but it is the seed of the green that I buy and we do not sow it (in a drill, outside) until late May or early June – making sure that the weather is propitious and that the ground is not wet and sticky. Given these conditions, we have, at least in recent summers, had great success with purslane at Dixter, finding it difficult to keep up with the crop, which you must do, by constantly picking the terminal, leafy shoots so as to encourage further shoot production from lower down.

Purslane: the whole young shoot is edible

Thin the seedlings to 6in apart. When signs of flowering become apparent, you should prevent them. We don't, and are sometimes able to save our own seed, which always gives a sense of satisfaction. The flowers, which open in the mornings, are tiny, yellow things.

This is a salad ingredient with a difference, and I recommend it highly, if your climate is reasonably warm in summer. On its own, the flavour is a little strange – kind of musty – but in a mixed salad that is not apparent.

Fennel

*T*here are several confusions over the identification of fennel. Giant fennel, *Ferula communis,* and other species of *Ferula,* are rarely eaten outside their countries of origin and have little aroma. They have magnificent foliage, however, and are wonderful ornamentals. *F. communis* rises to 9ft when flowering. Its growth period is from midwinter to midsummer, after which it becomes dormant: so you can plant late-flowering annuals around it. I have tall tulips among its foliage, in the spring. There are many other species, some tender, but many must be hardy, such as those from high up in Anatolia, where the winters are severe. We await their introduction, by seed, to this country. I saw them in eastern Turkey, in May, and they were already enticing beyond belief.

The strongly aromatic fennel is *Foeniculum vulgare.* It is naturalized in Britain, especially in chalky, maritime areas like Thanet, in East Kent. It is a fairly short-lived perennial, though you hardly notice this in the garden, as it self-sows so freely. The problem, there, is how to contain its abundance. The ordinary *F. vulgare* is green-leaved and about 6ft tall at flowering. At that time, in late July, it looks handsome combined with clumps of the fiery red montbretia *Crocosmia* 'Lucifer'.

A popular variant is 'Purpureum', the purple fennel, whose young foliage is mole-coloured. You can make an effective spring bedding scheme with year-old seedlings of this, interplanted with tall spring-flowering yellow tulips, such as the pale 'Niphetos'. At the end of its season, the foliage on this purple form can look tarnished, and the green type-plant may be preferable. As a general rule, you should try to remember to cut these fennels right down to the ground and to burn their tops, before they shed their ripe seed. They will make a cushion of young growth at the base, soon after this operation.

Aphids are apt to swarm over the young growth of fennel in May or June, and should be sprayed against, if necessary.

The aniseed aroma of these fennels' foliage can be made use of for garnishing fish, for instance. But the real meat of our subject, from the gastronomic viewpoint, is reached with the bulb fennel or Florence fennel, *Foeniculum vulgare* var. *dulce.* This is a stockier plant, wherein the leaf bases

Florence fennel, promising a good crop

are so swollen and fleshy as to make up a kind of bulb. Those plants that bolt before you can eat them will grow only up to 4ft high; and the yellow-green flowers are borne on wider inflorescences, making bold features when used in cut flower arrangements.

All the samples of this fennel that we buy ready for eating have been imported from warmer climates, and irrigation will have been plentifully supplied, so that the crop will grow fast and without stress. At Dixter, matters are a little trickier and the season is shorter, but excellent results can be obtained. I have been experimenting with Florence fennel for some years, making two or three direct sowings annually. If one goes wrong, another may succeed.

The ground needs to be fertile and moisture-retaining, with plenty of well-rotted bulky organic matter dug into it during the previous winter. Seed can be drilled at intervals, from late May to the end of August. Late-maturing crops have been among my most successful, as there is less urge for the plants to run up to flower. In a frost-free autumn, I have still been cutting good bulbs into November. The young plants should be thinned to not less than 9in in the row, so that there is no competition between them, otherwise bolting is much likelier before decent bulbs have been made. Bolting is also premature if the developing plants go short of water. While growing fast, they need this in abundance.

If you follow these instructions (and I don't, always, myself, life being full of distractions), you will be the proud producer of larger 'bulbs' than you have ever bought at a shop. If there's any danger of their not holding till you're ready to eat them, they should be cut at their peak and will keep well in a plastic bag in the refrigerator for several weeks.

In Salads

There is both crunch and substance in raw fennel. One, or even half a leaf base will contribute enough for quite a large green salad. Having washed it, I cut down the veins, to make slivers or scoops of fennel. Until you get near to the heart of the bulb, there is a good deal of stringy fibre on the outside of the leaf. This would largely (though not wholly) disappear, if cooked; but raw, it needs removing. So I break the pieces I have cut, outwards, towards the convex side, and then ease them apart. This exposes the fibre, whose removal can then be completed with a knife.

In a mixed salad, the heavy bits, like fennel or radish, will always drop to the bottom of the bowl when you are mixing in the vinaigrette dressing. Make sure that everyone helps themselves before it comes to your turn (*so* polite); then you'll be sure of a good share of the chunky bottom area of the salad.

COOKING FENNEL

Fennel becomes much milder when cooked, and you can eat ten times as much of it. It is not unusual to allow one bulb per person, if the bulbs are of moderate size. Your own, if you have been clever, will be immoderately large, but quite a few of the tougher, outer leaves (which are also the smallest) will be discarded. Trim off the top, close to the bulb. Make sure that no mud remains lodged between the leaf bases that remain. The two on the outside may be the better for de-stringing, without actually dislodging them from the solid base.

The simplest cooking method is to cut each bulb into four, first lengthways, then at right angles. You can do some more cleaning at this stage. Drop into boiling salted water and boil for 15 minutes. Drain; then to the same pan add a large knob of butter and, at a low temperature, continue to cook the fennel for a further 15 minutes, with the lid off, turning it in the butter. If you like, you can add grated Parmesan just before serving.

Alternatively, while the fennel is boiling, gently cook a chopped onion and a chopped clove of garlic in the knob of butter till soft, in a separate, covered pan. Add the drained fennel and more butter, and continue to cook, pan lid off. Cream may be added near the end. A good accompaniment to fish or chicken.

FENNEL SOUFFLÉ

An excellent recipe from *Jane Grigson's Vegetable Book*. This quantity serves 3 or 4.

1lb prepared fennel, quartered
A large knob of butter to cook the fennel
Salt, black pepper
1 teaspoon aniseed-flavour spirit (optional)
1–2 rounded tablespoons
grated Parmesan cheese
1 heaped tablespoon dry breadcrumbs

4 tablespoons butter
⅓ cup all-purpose flour
⅔ cup fennel cooking liquid
⅔ cup milk
4 egg yolks
Cayenne pepper
1 tablespoon chopped hazelnuts
1 tablespoon chopped fresh parsley
5 egg whites, stiffly beaten

211

Prepare a fennel purée by blanching the quartered fennel for 15 minutes in boiling salted water. Drain, reserving ⅔ cup of the cooking liquid. Stew the fennel in butter, lid off, for a further 10 minutes, until it is really soft. Purée in a blender or food processor. Season with salt and pepper, adding the aniseed-flavour spirit if you like, and 1 tablespoon of grated Parmesan.

Put a baking tray in the oven and pre-heat to 200°C/400°F/gas mark 6. Grease a 6-cup soufflé dish with a butter paper. Tip in crumbs and cheese and turn the dish about so that the sides and base are evenly coated; keep the surplus to one side.

Melt the 4 tablespoons of butter in a large pan, stir in the flour and leave it to cook for a few minutes. Moisten with the cooking liquid and the milk. Stir in the fennel purée. Remove the pan from the heat and whisk in the egg yolks, one by one. Season with salt, black pepper and a pinch of cayenne and add the hazelnuts and the parsley. The flavour should be on the strong side, as the egg whites will have the effect of toning it down. Fold in the stiffly beaten whites carefully, raising the mass with a metal spoon. Do not worry if all the white is not mixed smoothly in; a few smallish lumps matter less than losing too much air from the froth.

Spoon the soufflé mixture into the prepared dish. Sprinkle the surplus crumbs and cheese on top. Bake for 30 minutes.

FENNEL STUFFING FOR RIVER FISH

From Jane Grigson's *Fish Cookery:* 'Flavourings of the aniseed type go well with fish of all kinds. . . . Here's a mixture, a *battuto* from Italy, which can be used as a bed for baked fish, or as a stuffing, if breadcrumbs and egg are added.' This recipe is only enough for 4, I would say. Last evening I used this stuffing in the largest rainbow trout I have ever bought. Inviting four young friends in to share it (all of them originally met when students at Wye Horticultural College, Kent), there was still one-third of the fish left over. Yet we could have done with more stuffing. (A good stuffing, too, for chicken and turkey.)

3 slices *prosciutto* or lean smoked bacon
1 large clove of garlic
1 head of fennel
Olive oil or butter (or a mixture of the two)
1½ cups fresh breadcrumbs
1 egg, beaten

Chop the *prosciutto,* or bacon, with the garlic and fennel. Melt enough oil or butter to cover the base of a skillet thinly, and stew the chopped mixture in it over a low heat, until the fennel softens. Don't let it brown. Add the breadcrumbs and the beaten egg. Season well.

After stuffing the trout, I wrapped it loosely in foil, together with four bulbs of fennel, quartered and pre-cooked for 15 minutes in boiling, salted water. There was also butter and olive oil added to the foil parcel. The baking time, at 230°C/450°F/gas mark 8, was 50 minutes.

While this was cooking, we started with the tomato dish on page 216, but this could well have accompanied the fish, the tomato colour, as well as contents, being an asset.

Tomato

I grow some tomatoes in the garden every year; none under glass. Those would be hopelessly neglected. In summer and early autumn, all our thoughts are outside.

This is one of the most beautiful and enticing of fruits and the orange colouring is, one has to admit, too large a part of its attraction. The buyer is beguiled by looks alone and, all too often, fails to take notice of very poor flavour. Dutch and English tomatoes grown under glass are not worth eating from the time they first come in, in spring, till late summer. Then they do achieve *some* flavour, despite the grower's aim, heavily abetted by his manurial programme, to obtain a large crop. Large crops rarely go hand in hand with flavour. Even though you can buy special packs of 'Gardener's Delight' in the supermarkets, their flavour and sweetness won't begin to compare with what you can produce from your own garden.

If the tomatoes from your garden have failed (I am ashamed to say mine often have), then buy in September and early October from a farm shop where perfection has not been – I won't say, the primary aim – but has yielded, in some degree, to human fallibility. That way you'll be buying a more naturally produced fruit, with character and aroma. For much of the year, fresh tomatoes comprise only a small part of my shopping list. For cooking, tinned Italian tomatoes, grown where summer sunshine is abundant, will have the flavour you are looking for.

One's own produce is a special treat, though I have yet to find the ideal garden variety for my south of England climate (and I can't really complain about that). 'Gardener's Delight' is certainly a must, unless I forsake it for 'Sungold', which is even sweeter, but still marble-sized; a larger fruit is frequently a lot more useful. 'Alicante', an old variety, is medium-sized and can give satisfaction; I still grow that and I have a stab at a large-fruited, beefsteak (once known as oxheart) type. 'Marmande' is geared to outdoor living. It's an ugly fruit and rarely ripens to a heavy crop. The growth habit is awkward – what's known as determinate. Having reached a height, up your supporting cane, of 15in or a little more, it stops. You have to train its topmost side-shoot upwards. That wastes precious time.

'Alicante' has the more usual, indeterminate, habit of growth. You keep on tying the same shoot to its stout cane, or other support, removing once a week

213

Young salad tomatoes, not yet ripening

all side-shoots that would otherwise compete. Eventually, about the end of summer, you stop (pinch out) the main shoot so that all the plant's energies can concentrate on swelling and ripening the fruitlets that are already there.

Bush tomatoes are a third kind and popular with some gardeners (not with me), on account of needing no support. They branch continually and grovel around at ground level getting muddy and are a prey to slug damage. You can straw them to keep them clean, as you would strawberries, but that further encourages slugs. No bush tomato makes fruit of any size.

I have grown the yellow 'Golden Sunrise' on a number of occasions. It is good-tempered and free-fruiting but small, and its thin skin means that it soon shrivels after picking. It is a wet and watery fruit. Also, I do prefer the orange colouring of a traditional tomato. 'Golden Sunrise' is a bit anaemic.

A mixture of 'Sungold', 'Alicante' and 'Highlander' tomatoes

214

C U L T I V A T I N G   T O M A T O E S

Tomato seed is pale and furry and has great survival powers. It passes intact through the long human alimentary canal. The sewage sludge that farmers buy from sewage farms and thereafter stack (not too near to a dwelling, one hopes), will shortly afterwards sprout all over with tomato seedlings. Seed that you buy will remain viable for at least three years, if you keep it in a cool place. As you'll need only a few plants of each variety you grow, sow a small amount and keep the rest.

Early April is soon enough to sow, under cold glass. Bring the seedlings on, still under glass, potting them individually, and harden them off completely, well before planting out in early June. Soil-borne diseases afflict tomatoes, so you should give them a change of position each year, the sunnier the better. If on the dry side, the fruit flavour will be all the better, though extra water may need to be applied while the first trusses are swelling. A spacing of 15in between plants is generally enough if the row is unshaded on either side. Make sure the support is strong enough to carry the crop when it is heavy, in September. Pick the fruit as soon as it begins to colour and finish it off indoors.

Although it is lovely to pick unsprayed fruit and to eat it (in the case of 'Gardener's Delight' and 'Sungold') straight off the bush, one simply cannot ignore the danger from potato blight. Protective sprays of fungicide need to be applied every ten days or so, from the end of July. Once the fungus is in the plant, there'll be no recovery.

T O M A T O E S   S T U F F E D   W I T H
A N C H O V Y - F L A V O U R E D   B R E A D C R U M B S

Serve as a first course, or, as suggested on page 212, it would also be a good accompaniment to a main-course fish dish.

6 large tomatoes
2 small (2oz) cans of anchovies, drained
and chopped
1 clove of garlic, chopped
A handful of pimento-stuffed olives, sliced
1–1½ cups fresh breadcrumbs

Preheat the oven to 200°C/400°F/ gas mark 6.

Cut off the tops of the tomatoes, setting the tops aside to make lids. Scoop out the middle of the tomatoes, removing the core and seeds; discard. Mix together the anchovies, garlic, olives and breadcrumbs and use this mixture to stuff the tomatoes.

Arrange the tomatoes, lids restored, in a gratin dish. Bake for 20 minutes.

LOTTE EN GIGOT

Lotte en Gigot, from Jane Grigson's *Fish Cookery*, is one of my favourites and I was cooking it last evening, before writing this chapter. Because of illness, we were only three, and I had bought a 2½lb tailpiece of monkfish from Johnny Swann, my favourite fishmonger, from the group of small shops on the front at old Hastings, the day before. Nevertheless, we finished the lot(te). There was quite enough for five normal servings. For extra vegetables we had steamed leeks ('Winter Crop'), and my own 'Pink Fir Apple' potatoes, boiled in their skins and then peeled very quickly. We followed up with *Gooseberry Fool* (see page 84).

We are told that this is a popular French recipe, which can also be used for other firm fish. The *lotte* is described as *en gigot* because its tailpiece shape is reminiscent of a leg of lamb.

2½–3lb tailpiece of monkfish
6 tablespoons olive oil
Salt and pepper
½ cup warm water (I normally
use half as much)

Sauce
2lb tomatoes, peeled and chopped
½ cup olive oil
2 cloves garlic, chopped

1 tablespoon chopped fresh parsley
1lb mushrooms, washed and quartered
(if using large mushrooms, slice them thinly
in opposite directions)
Salt and pepper
1½ cups heavy cream
Lemon juice
Extra parsley

Preheat the oven to 220°C/425°F/gas mark 7. Put the fish into a presentable baking dish, pour oil over it, and season. Cook in the hot oven for 15 minutes, then turn the heat down to 180°C/350°F/gas mark 4. Add the water and leave for another 30 minutes, basting from time to time (unless you're with your guests, enjoying a drink).

Meanwhile, make the sauce: cook the tomatoes in half the oil until they are reduced to a thick purée; add the garlic and parsley. At the same time, in another pan, cook the mushrooms in the rest of the oil. Season.

When the fish is just done, take it from the oven and turn the temperature up again to 220°C/425°F/gas mark 7. Stir the tomatoes, mushrooms and cream together and pour over the fish. Add the lemon juice and more seasoning, and return to the hot oven for 5 minutes. Serve in the cooking dish and sprinkle with parsley.

RIPE TOMATO CHUTNEY

Many of the friends who visit me in autumn will bring a gift of their own green tomato chutney. This is the result of not wanting to 'waste' the abundance of green outdoor tomatoes that they are left with after the first frost. I find it revolting. (Perhaps they do, too.)

This recipe for a ripe tomato chutney (which I quoted in *A Year at Great Dixter*), is a very different matter and, at my table, is a regular accompaniment to cold meats and green salad. My mother had it from a friend in our village. The fruit should be prepared before weighing. These quantities make about 13lb.

4lb apples, peeled, cored and sliced
6lb ripe tomatoes
4lb soft brown sugar
3 cups golden raisins
3½ tablespoons salt
1 tablespoon ground ginger
1 teaspoon cayenne pepper (I use less)

Scant 1 cup finely chopped onions
or shallots
5 cups malt vinegar

Cook the apples first, separately. Skin the tomatoes after pouring boiling water over them, in a bowl. Chop them roughly. Put all the ingredients in a preserving pan and boil for an hour or more, until the mixture thickens to the extent that it erupts and makes small craters, like lava in a volcano. Pot in clean, broad-mouthed jars, covering with double layers of waxed paper. Store in a cool place.

PORK CASSEROLE

This is one of my most-used recipes. Casseroles are such a boon for not demanding last-minute attention. Serves 4.

2lb shoulder of pork, cut into cubes
2 tablespoons olive oil
2 onions, sliced
1 rounded tablespoon all-purpose flour
1lb tomatoes, peeled and chopped, or one
One 14oz tin of chopped tomatoes
¾ cup red wine
2 cloves of garlic, chopped
1 teaspoon dried basil (I preserve
my own fresh basil)
Salt and pepper
½ cup pimento-stuffed olives cut in
half transversely

Heat the oil in a large, heavy-based casserole set over a medium heat. Add the cubes of pork, enough at a time to cover the base, and brown them on all sides, removing each batch to a plate as it's done. Then add the onions to the pan and soften them in the oil for a few minutes. Return the browned meat to the pan and sprinkle in the flour.

Stir well and add the chopped tomatoes. Pour in the wine, add the garlic and basil and season with salt and pepper. Stir. Bring slowly to simmering point, then cover the pan and put it in the oven. Cook the casserole at 140°C/275°F/gas mark 1 for 1½ hours. Add the olives, cover again and cook for another 30 minutes.

Rocket

*I*t is only in recent years that we have heard of rocket in England, yet it has been one of my top favourite salad ingredients for quite a while now. You will even find it in the supermarkets, at a high price and with scarcely any flavour – but still, it is there.

There is a confusion over its name. The edible rocket of which I write is *Eruca sativa*, a cruciferous annual from the Mediterranean, which in America is known as arugula. It is doubtless with an eye on the American markets that it is so listed in Thompson & Morgan's seed catalogue. Confusion might further arise with sweet rocket, another crucifer, but an ornamental, short-lived perennial, grown for its pinky-mauve or pure white flowers, in spring, and having a delicious night fragrance. I don't suppose it is poisonous but it is never eaten.

Eruca sativa has a leaf resembling watercress (for which it is sometimes used as a substitute). It is extremely popular with flea beetle and is riddled with holes made by that insect all through the summer. Additionally, in summer, it runs quickly to flower

and seed. The white flowers are perfectly edible, but there is often little left to eat. However, you should let some of your rocket plants run to seed, as you'll never have enough from packets, even though you buy three of them each year, as I do. You can collect some of your ripe rocket seed and allow the rest to self-sow.

Your best crops will be from September to April. Make a sowing, broadcast or in a row in late August, thinning the seedlings to 9in. Given an open autumn, rocket will come on so that you are picking leaves from October. Provided the plants remain in a reasonably youthful condition, they will survive quite hard winter weather, but if already stemmy and flowering when the cold arrives, they may suffer terminally. We also make an early spring sowing and have joy from that for a few weeks.

Pick the young leaves as they develop and also pick young shoots that are running to flower buds, or are even flowering. So long as they are tender, they will, roughly chopped, mix into your salads and add a wonderful cress flavour with quite a bite to it but not harsh or coarse like land cress.

Radish

R adish seeds are among the first given to children by parents wanting to get them interested in growing things. Summer radishes develop with amazing speed – a mere three or four weeks between sowing and harvesting – if not overcrowded and if plenty of moisture is available. With their red skins and white insides, they are pretty.

I don't bother with them, because the moment of being pleasantly edible is so short. In next to no time, as they age, they become disconcertingly hot. It is, of course, easy to buy them at the right stage, but there is a pulpiness of consistency in the summer radishes on offer, which is disappointing when you know how crisp they can be.

More to the point are the *hardy* winter radishes, which, from a midsummer sowing, remain in good eating condition throughout the winter months, though slug damage is a hazard. I have a lot, yet, to learn about winter radishes, but I keep trying varieties that are new to me. Even those that become large

In spring, the shoots on a winter radish burst into flower

remain quite mild-flavoured. In February, I had a 'Black Spanish Round' radish, the size of a large turnip, black-skinned and white inside. Its texture was coarse and I do not rate it highly for its root. But it was already making new shoots, preparatory to flowering, and these were mild and tender and suitable for green salads. Later, they were produced in great abundance and cooked well as a green vegetable. Another winter radish (name lost), with a red skin and white interior, is not large at all, and the young (flowering) shoots on that were very tasty raw.

IN SALADS

To quote Joy Larkcom in *The Salad Garden*: 'The seed pods of any radishes that have run to seed can be eaten in salads, but the larger the radish, the larger, the more succulent, and the tastier the pods. They can be very pleasantly spicy. Whether being used fresh or pickled, they should be picked when still young enough to snap crisply in two.'

Flowers

No salad looks more attractive than when finished off, over its surface, with a scattering of edible flowers. The guests who are not used to this embellishment will sedulously avoid helping themselves to such foreign bodies or, if unavoidable, will leave them on the side of their plate. But in my house, they are in a very small minority.

Flowers, or parts of flowers, are generally fragile. If you can pick them clean and avoid the need to wash, and hence to bruise, them, that is the ideal. And your salad dressing must be mixed in before the flowers are sprinkled on, at the last moment. I try to gather them, or get a fellow enthusiast to do so for me, at the last moment, too, so that all is fresh.

Primroses, whether typically pale yellow or coloured, are often available right through a mild winter, but really come into their own in March and April. They are sweet to taste and can be gathered with the green calyx, which is perfectly palatable.

Flowers to ornament a salad: primroses, borage and sweet-scented violets

The leaves of nasturtiums are hot and rank, but the flowers are excellent in salads

Sweet-scented violets are for early spring, too. Although they are typically violet in colour, you should also make sure of growing pink, white and even pale yellow varieties. The last is *Viola* 'Sulphurea'; it flowers a little later than the others. Primroses and violets flourish underneath deciduous shrubs, flowering before these have come into leaf and happy to be in dense shade during the summer.

The pot marigold, *Calendula officinalis*, will self-sow, once you have it; and overwintered plants start flowering as early as April. They gradually return to their single-flowered state, over the years, but as you pull off their rays and use them alone, their lack of sophistication will not be observed. The bright orange colouring is really cheerful. You need something blue to go with it. Borage is good, but I tend to lose it after a few years, unless I renew the stock. Generally I have *Anchusa azurea,* which flowers from May on. Young plants will also be flowering in the autumn. Just pull the corolla out of its hairy, green calyx. If you have old roots around of endive, their flowers are a marvellous, pure shade of blue. They flower only in the morning, so are no use for an evening meal. In any case, blue is grey by artificial light. Salsify is another morning-flowerer, purple in colouring.

In summer, the pink or mauve heads of chives in flower are tender and edible. Nasturtiums offer a wide range of colours. They are popular with pollen beetles, after the oil-seed rape has finished flowering. Sometimes these insects

Day lily, Hemerocallis fulva

reach such plague numbers that it is impossible to shake them all out of the cupped base of the nasturtium blooms.

Elderflowers have a strong personality (see pages 247–9); they are popular with insects, too. Rose petals, wild or cultivated, are excellent. I wouldn't like to say which are the best, though one would imagine those with the best scent. Day lily buds, the day before they burst into flower, are deliciously crunchy, though not in all varieties. The best is *Hemerocallis fulva,* and the double-flowered form of that, best of all. The flavour is of green figs. As the buds are large, I should chop them into segments.

The flowers of scented-leaved 'geraniums' (pelargoniums) are good, I am told, though I have not used them. Clearly there is plenty of scope for experimentation, short of careless poisoning.

HERBS

Parsley

Mint

Chives

Chervil

Basil

Dill

Lovage

Tarragon

Bay Laurel

Rosemary

Sage

Thyme

Savory

Elderflower

Herbs

The herb garden or herb patch is one of our most popular garden features. It is often designed in a formal pattern and will include many plants that serve no culinary purpose. It generally looks passable, even pretty, in early summer, but thereafter gets completely out of hand, ending up a fearful mess – like the bedrooms of its owners, I suspect.

This is because many herbs are of weedy habit and are, indeed, weeds at heart. Their foliage is not beautiful – think of tarragon, for instance, and basil; they run around by suckering – mint; or they are mad self-sowers – fennel. If you put them all together, it is hard to disguise their aesthetic failings for long.

However, various pretty forms of herbs that originally had no pretensions to beauty have been developed, either with larger and more colourful flowers or with coloured foliage. Where this has not been detrimental to their services as potherbs, those are the ones to grow. A herb bed will almost certainly look its best in the second season after planting. Following that, rapid deterioration will set in and I would recommend that you replant all of its herbaceous contents every third year. Split them and replant in improved soil. A certain amount of self-seeding, as of borage, is charming, but always exercise a vigilant eye and a restraining hand.

I like to have most of the herbs that I regularly use growing near to the kitchen, but they are scattered around, for all that. In this way you can indulge their preferences – thyme, for instance, seeds itself into the cracks of a drystone wall – while mitigating the impact of their off-periods. The plants of different genera vary enormously in size, from a full-grown bay laurel down. That again suggests the choice of varying habitats. One character that most of them do share is a strong preference for sunshine and good drainage.

HERBS IN SALADS

In salads I use, as available, a few leaves of chervil, a couple of dill, one of sorrel (*or* one of spinach); sometimes a tiny part of a leaf of lovage and a tiny shoot, chopped, of tarragon. But all this is according to individual taste.

PAGE 226 *Flowering chives*
PAGE 227 *Chervil*
OPPOSITE *Thyme in flower; it sows itself in a wall near the kitchen*

BOUQUET GARNI

The *bouquet garni*, used to give a herby flavour to fish and meat stocks, sauces, gravies and stews, varies a little according to the time of year and, hence, availability. I do not differentiate on account of what it is to accompany, except that I use a bay leaf only where a strong extra flavour is required. I rarely use rosemary because of its over-affectionate sweetness. The herbs I draw on are:

parsley (stems)
chervil (leaf with stem)
basil (shoot)
dill (leaf)
bay leaf (small)
tarragon (sprig)
thyme (sprig)
winter savory (sprig)
celeriac (stem) *or*
lovage (leaflet – in spring and early summer)
sorrel (a flowering stem is good)

I tie a good piece of string around the stems or leaves, leaving plenty to spare at the free end, so that it dangles outside the receptacle in which the *bouquet* is included. This enables the *bouquet* to be extracted easily when its duty is done, and I save the string to serve many turns.

Parsley

As being the most important herb, I will start here. Parsley is either grown principally for looks (curly-leaved) or principally for flavour (flat- or plain-leaved). The uses of 'for-looks' parsley can be sub-divided as (1) to garnish food produced in the kitchen – I can scarcely ever be bothered to do this – and (2) to ornament the garden.

Parsley, *Petroselinum crispum*, is a biennial. It is of such continuous, year-round value in the kitchen, finding a place, chopped up, in the vast proportion of savoury dishes, that I would recommend three sowings. That is, of the flat-leaved kind, which has much the strongest and best flavour.

First, I sow a pinch of seed in a pot, in March and under cold glass. The seedlings are then potted off individually and subsequently planted. They have a head start over the next sowing, which will be direct, in late April or May, in a drill where the crop will be required to grow. Should either of these sowings run out of steam, or be too soft and flabby to survive the winter, a third sowing, in June, is to be recommended, again into the open ground, watering

Flat-leaved parsley

the bottom of the drill just before sowing, if the weather is dry. But in any case, choose a well-dug, moisture-retaining piece of ground.

You will usually find yourself either with more parsley than you can possibly want or with none at all. The above procedure will avoid the indignity of the second condition for most of the time, but parsley is not altogether hardy and you may lose your crop in a hard winter. In that case you'll be buying imported stuff, sold by weight and apparently bred specifically to have heavy, thick stems rather than abundance of leaf blade. Stems are all very well for a *bouquet garni* or for making stock and I chop some up to include in my dogs' lunches, but an excess of stem is a cheat.

Parsley with curly leaves may vary a lot in appearance from plant to plant. A seed strain ('Bravour' is one that has given me level results in the past) may make its debut in award-winning form, but is liable to deteriorate over the years, once released to the trade by the breeder.

A good curled parsley can be a smashing bedding plant, as its colouring is a particularly vivid shade of green and will contrast excitingly with a bright orange dwarf marigold (*Tagetes*) such as 'Disco Orange'. However, parsley plants sometimes run into trouble from virus disease (spread by aphids). The foliage turns pink and the plant dies. As well, then, to have some spares available, either in pots or in the open ground, as parsley will transplant if you are careful about it, watering heavily both before and after the operation.

In Cooking

I usually serve boiled gammon (smoked and on the bone, for best flavour) with parsley sauce (see page 147). A simple and satisfying dish that is always popular.

Parsley can be added, chopped, just before serving to most vegetable soups: lentil, cucumber (see page 200), zucchini, celery and cheese, carrot (Crécy, see page 103), nettle, salsify. Or, sprinkled over completed fish dishes, such as turbot or brill fillets with shrimp or prawn sauce, or with vermouth on a bed of parsley and chopped shallots, or with orange sauce; or whiting fillets with orange sauce; or monkfish recipes. It can also be chopped over the celery to finish pheasant braised with celery; or used in parsley and lemon stuffing (with white bread) for turkey.

Mint

Two species of mint are most commonly used for culinary purposes: spearmint, *Mentha spicata*, smooth and with sharply pointed leaves, is the one I was brought up on. But for many years now I have preferred apple mint, which has rounded, softly furry leaves. Traditionalists are put off by the fur, but this disappears completely when the mint is chopped up.

Mint plants are travellers, always seeking pastures new. They never remain for long where planted, but quest ever outwards. This can be a great nuisance when neighbouring plants are invaded. It is a good plan to replant at frequent intervals, early spring being the best time to make a new bed. This is easily done with the underground rhizomes, every piece of which will make a new plant. Growing mint boxed in, so that it cannot stray, may sound a good idea but the cabined plant quickly starves, and should be replanted annually in fresh soil.

You should be in fresh mint from mid-spring into autumn. When the main shoots show flower buds, pinch them out (these tips can be used) and the plant will react by making young side growths. If you fail to do this, the whole plant will harden and the season will be much curtailed.

IN COOKING

A sprig of mint adds fresh flavour to boiling new potatoes and green peas. I always like to make fresh mint sauce to go with roast lamb (substituting redcurrant jelly in the mint's off-season). But mint sauce, as you all too often meet it, with a few chopped leaves swimming in a mass of malt vinegar, is abominable and death to the flavour of any red wine that may accompany the meal.

MINT SAUCE

Chop finely a handful of fresh mint leaves. Put them in a mortar with one or two tablespoons of sugar (according to taste) and pound with the pestle. Allow this mixture to rest for half an hour or so. Then add wine vinegar. I like a pretty solid sauce, so I add only so much as will just appear at the surface of the mint-and-sugar mix.

233

MINT ICE-CREAM

This is a bit of trouble but good for a party. It is another recipe given me by Michael Schuster. Serves 12, approximately.

1¼ cups superfine sugar
1¼ cups water
2 handfuls of mint leaves
Juice of 1 lemon
2½ cups heavy cream

Dissolve the sugar in the water slowly at first, then bring to the boil. Put the mint leaves in a blender, add the hot syrup and blend for several minutes or until the mint is well chopped. Leave to cool and then strain into a mixing bowl.

Add the lemon juice and cream to the cold syrup and whisk to blend the ingredients. Cover and place in the freezer. Remove after 3 hours and beat till the mixture is homogenized. Return to the freezer for another 3 hours.

Before serving, remove from the freezer and leave at room temperature. The time depends on your living temperature – it may need an hour, as this is a dense mix and takes longer to soften than most ice-creams. Turn out into a serving bowl.

ABOVE *Gathering mint tips*
LEFT *Apple mint running through drystone walling (some shoot tips already picked)*

Chives

When I was younger, the normally grown form of chives was a small, fine-textured plant with squinny little flower heads. This was *Allium schoenoprasum. A. s. sibiricum*, a plant larger in all its parts and with showy, rather scabious-like flower heads, was known as giant chives. Nowadays, only giant chives are grown, under the name of *A. schoenoprasum*, and *sibiricum* appears to have been dropped.

These are eye-catching plants, well deserving a front-line position in any border and making their greatest display in May. The flower heads vary in colouring between mauve and pink. Two of the pinkest, namely 'Black Isle Blush' and (yet another) 'Pink Perfection', developed by Poyntsfield Herb Nursery, Black Isle, Dingwall, Ross and Cromarty, have been given the Award of Garden Merit. (Of the cherry tree given the name 'Pink Perfection', Collingwood Ingram observed that it sounded like a spoiled child in need of a spanking.)

Chives are found in various forms over a large part of the old world and are perfectly hardy perennials, dying down in late autumn but reappearing as early as the end of January, in a mild winter. They make dense clumps and the stems are so thin, even at the base, as scarcely to constitute bulbs.

Overcrowding results in a diminution of leaf and flower size. Clumps should be divided and reset in improved soil every third year or oftener. After flowering, it is advisable to slash the plants right back to ground level (a few swipes with a large old kitchen knife does the job perfectly) before their seed ripens, as self-sown seedlings can be numerous and tiresome. New growth will appear within days and will be young and fresh for use. There will be further flowers on a more half-hearted scale and a second slash-back should follow.

IN SALADS AND COOKING

Chives, always used fresh, make an excellent last-minute addition to soups, in particular lentil soup with cream, sorrel soup (page 203) and spinach soup. I don't usually add chives to my mixed salads, though it makes a nice change when a guest makes a salad for me. Good with baked beets (page 108)

Young chive leaves

and potato salad (page 114), too.

When the shoots are young, I love thin sandwiches filled with a mixture of cream cheese and chives, seasoned with salt and pepper.

Chervil

There are not so many salad ingredients that can be used from the garden all through the cold months, but chervil, *Anthriscus cerefolium*, is one of them. Related to parsley but with a distinct aniseed flavour, chervil is a hardy annual that grows best in cool weather. The leaves are pinnately divided and arise from a central crown. An early spring sowing, either broadcast or in a short row, will provide you with leaves in early summer, after which running to seed becomes a problem and I find it best to delay the next sowing till late summer, to provide plants for use from autumn to spring. Growth slows down considerably during winter but can be coaxed along by the use of cloches.

Chervil's aniseed flavour makes it a perfect addition to mixed salads. Combined with chopped tarragon, parsley and chives, it is a component of the *fines herbes* of French cookery, notably as a flavouring for an omelette.

Basil

I frequently have to resort to dried basil, as I often fail to grow decent plants, but in this I am improving. The secret, I believe, is to assume that the plant is quite tender. It easily rots if the weather is chilly and damp. There are quite a number of varieties. Bush basil and sweet basil make a good contrast.

Sow in a pot under glass – it can be unheated, if you wait until late spring. Prick out the seedlings and finally pot them individually. If growing well, a 6in pot will not be too large. I stand a couple of these pots against the warm wall just outside my kitchen. They need watering every two or three days. The rest are kept in a cold greenhouse.

Basil has an affinity with tomato, either in a salad or in stews and sauces.

Dill

Closely related to fennel, the main difference in dill is that it is an annual. This means that its main object in life is to flower and set seed. Coming from southern Europe, where it is often a weed of cultivation, it is not hardy in Britain.

The trouble is that dill is often not there when you want it. Sow it little and often, in short rows, starting in spring, and thinning the seedlings to 6–8in apart. The plants are naturally thin and spindly and remain on one stem that branches little. Late sowings in September are a good idea, as the plants are slower running to flower during the autumn season. If frost holds off, you may still be picking fresh leaves into winter. You needn't be in a hurry to clear away plants that have run to seed, as self-sown seedlings will come as a pleasant surprise, just when you'd thought you'd run out.

IN SALADS AND COOKING

I use the feathery foliage, which is an excellent flavouring, chopped fine, in mixed salads.

Chopped dill goes well in a potato salad. It is also an excellent companion to cucumber. (In the cucumber soup recipe given on page 200, you can substitute dill for parsley.) Like fennel, it goes well with fish, especially salmon.

Lovage

There is a confusion of names, here, which took me a long while to unravel. The British native lovage, *Ligusticum scoticum* (it grows on Scottish coastlines, including Orkney), is a nice-looking plant, only 2ft high with umbels of white blossom (for this is another member of Umbelliferae). However, although edible, this is not the potherb that we grow as lovage. That is *Levisticum officinale*, a perennial from the Mediterranean, though perfectly hardy. *Levisticum*, it seems, is a corruption of *Ligusticum*. You know what copy typists are.

Seed of the potherb is said to germinate best from an autumn sowing, but is perfectly satisfactory, in my experience, sown in a pot in spring and later transplanted to its permanent position. As it makes a leggy and undistinguished plant when flowering (not at all like any of the fennels), I shouldn't include it in a herb garden for display. Still, it needs to be reasonably near the kitchen. Lovage is early into new leaf, in spring, at which time the young foliage is bronze. Quite nice to be overpowered by nibbling the corner of a leaflet.

IN SALADS AND COOKING

Lovage has a very strong flavour of celery and only a little should be used at a time; but that little is extremely useful when no leaves of celery or celeriac are available to give that flavour to stocks or salads or to a *bouquet garni* (see page 230). Joy Larkcom recommends (in *The Salad Garden*) rubbing a leaf against the inside of a wooden salad bowl. Mingled with many a squeeze of garlic from yesteryear, of course, and other nostalgic flavours. I again confess to preferring a ceramic bowl!

Tarragon

Tarragon is a herb that does nothing for the appearance of your patch; a mousy sort of plant, devoid of personality, with small, smooth lance leaves and flowers that never take off. That's just on the surface. As soon as you start to handle tarragon, you appreciate that it has breeding. The aroma is satisfyingly pervasive.

It is an artemisia, and all artemisias are aromatic. From our point of view, there are two kinds: the French, which is 2ft tall, apt to disappear, and highly aromatic; and the Russian, 3ft tall, hardy, and relatively weak on aroma. It is the former that you need to own and grow. It will survive a hard winter, but then disappear after a mild one. Poor drainage is the most likely reason. It hates to be waterlogged; on the other hand, it doesn't like to be dry and parched, either. If you give it a dry spot, add lots of organic goodies to the soil before planting.

Tarragon spreads into a patch by means of rhizomes, and the best way to increase it on a small scale is by detaching a few of these in early spring, when they break cleanly away from their point of origin. You can plant them where you want them or, for best results, pot them up in a light compost and establish them in a cold frame, before planting out. Cuttings of young shoots also root easily, in a close frame.

You can start using your tarragon in April. Picked fairly hard, up to midsummer, it will keep on putting out soft new shoots. Otherwise, the branching stems will harden and make flower buds. These retain the flavour but are not good for chopping up finely. But for tarragon chicken, for instance, you can go on picking sprays from the garden into late autumn, if frost holds off. It is always a good idea to replant some of your stock each spring.

TARRAGON CHICKEN

This is cooked in a casserole. I have quite a big, heavy one into which I can fit two birds, side by side, if they weigh no more than 3lb each. That's enough to feed eight. Or one fowl for four.

Brown the bird(s) in butter with a little olive oil to prevent the butter burning. Towards the end of browning, add one or two sliced onions or shallots. Then a glass of dry white wine and several branches of tarragon – a couple stuffed inside the cavity of each bird and a couple more along-side them. Be generous.

Cover and place in a preheated oven at 230°C/450°F/gas mark 8 for 40 minutes. Transfer the birds to a dish, remove the tarragon branches and finish off the gravy on the stovetop with a lump of fresh butter and mixed, chopped-up herbs – parsley, tarragon, sorrel, chervil, dill, rocket, a lovage leaflet, one shoot each of thyme and winter savory – a selection of any of these available. Just stir them in and that's it.

Bay Laurel

This is the true laurel, from the Mediterranean, with which wreaths were made to crown poets and victors in battle. Hence, *Laurus nobilis*. As an 'edible' herb, it differs materially from other shrubs loosely termed laurel, all of which are poisonous. Bay is a very strong flavour. You don't want it all the time, and when you do, pick a small leaf rather than a large! It is most used in stews and stocks.

The bay makes a large, many-stemmed and somewhat suckering shrub which may attain the stature of a tree, even in places where it is not altogether hardy. I have seen mine temporarily crippled by a hard winter and taking on such a

241

frightful appearance that I have to resist the temptation to cut everything to the ground: new shoots will undoubtedly be sent up from ground level, but they will be so soft as to be particularly vulnerable during the next winter. Better to cut back to some stout main stems. Although these may look inanimate, the chances are that by July they will start to sprout young shoots.

Bay laurels are often grown as topiary specimens in tubs, to mark an urban house entrance. Besides the ugliness of seeing a large leaf sliced with shears, such plants are particularly vulnerable to pests – scale insects and the bay sucker – which deform new growth and leave a sticky deposit on the foliage. This in turn becomes covered with self-descriptive sooty moulds. Unpruned free-standing trees, around which plenty of air circulates, are seldom affected.

Bay green is a warm shade, which looks cheerful above all in winter. My bay trees flower in May and the male tree makes quite a show, with massed yellow stamens, scented on the air if this is warm. Bees love them. The females make black fruits, like small damsons. They are freely distributed by birds, and I am always finding bird-sown seedlings from my neighbour's female bushes.

There is a golden-leaved form of bay, 'Aurea', which can look handsome if

Bay laurel before flowering

provided with the right background. And the narrow-leaved *Laurus nobilis* f. *angustifolia* is good, also.

Rosemary

There are a great many varieties of rosemary (*Rosmarinus officinalis*), of varying hardiness. None are fully hardy, but many will give you a pleasant surprise by surviving a hard winter, especially if growing on light, well-drained soil. The top of a retaining wall is ideal. As the shrub ages, it subsides into a condition of semi-collapse, with a bony structure. That can be charming, if you are not too much of the neat and tidy persuasion: but space should be allowed for the collapsed condition to develop without getting in the way. If neatness is important – for instance where rosemary is required to flank and mark the top of steps on either side – 'Miss Jessopp's Upright' will be the one to go for, but its flower colouring is weak and pasty.

There are numerous strains of prostrate rosemary. They can, as seen in the south of France, for instance, make a great curtain of growth down the face of a high retaining wall. They are mostly too tender for any but the mildest of climates; this is not always the case, though, and it is worth making enquiries of suppliers as to how hardy the strain offered is considered to be. Of a procumbent, semi-prostrate habit is 'Severn Sea', and its flowers are well coloured.

I grow Collingwood Ingram's introduction from Corsica, called 'Benenden Blue'. Vita Sackville-West gave me my original cuttings, which she had from him. I have found this to be as hardy as any rosemary around. The leaves are fine and linear, while the flowers, abundantly produced May, are a bright shade of mid-blue (always with a tinge of mauve).

Like most herbs, rosemary requires full sun. It is easily propagated from cuttings of young shoot tips, beginning to harden, in late summer or early autumn.

The aroma of rosemary is sweet and insistent. I occasionally include it in a *bouquet garni,* but do not otherwise bring it into my kitchen. Some people like to insert slivers of rosemary under the skin of lamb that is to be roasted. I do not think that is a good idea at all.

PAGE 244 *The fine-leaved rosemary* Rosmarinus officinalis *'Benenden Blue'*
PAGE 245 *A bee enjoying the flowers of winter savory*

Sage

Like bay, another strong, coarse flavour with which you need to be sparing. This is *Salvia officinalis*, but it has an enormous number of variants. The sage we grew when I was a child, was an extremely dull, scraggy shrub which never flowered, that I can remember. However, there are charmingly free-flowering forms which, as herbs, are just as potent. (One might as well combine business with pleasure, where possible.) The narrow-leaved one that I grow is called *S. lavandulifolia*.

Sage's only cultural requirements are good drainage and a sunny situation. See page 60 for my use of sage in *Applesauce*.

Thyme

Of the numerous species and varieties of thyme, *Thymus vulgaris* is the traditional one for culinary purposes. It makes a small, sprawling bush about 9in high and is smothered with clusters of pale mauve flowers in May – charming at the top of a retaining wall or ledge (which is the kind of well-drained situation it fancies), with a mat of *Phlox douglasii*, in the same colouring and flowering at the same time, to keep it company.

'Silver Posie', which is a yellow-variegated form, makes a pretty alternative to *T. vulgaris* straight. The latter self-sows quite freely, giving you automatic replacements when scraggy old plants need replacing

Thyme is a fundamental constituent of the *bouquet garni* and is also included in many casserole recipes. But I find its flavour rather on the sweet side and often replace it with winter savory.

Savory

Two kinds of savory, the summer (*Satureia hortensis*) and the winter (*S. montana*), are popular in the kitchen. Summer savory is an annual, sown in April. Its season is limited but it dries well. I seldom grow it.

Winter savory is a long-lived shrublet, having the same habit and preference for sun and sharp drainage as common thyme. I use it constantly. Its clustered leafy shoots consist of rather hard, linear, shiny leaves. In late spring, it runs up with soft shoots to produce its off-white flowers. It is easily rooted in autumn from cuttings of the overwintering shoots.

IN SALADS AND COOKING

The flavour of winter savory is less insipid than that of thyme. Chopped fine, it is an ingredient in omelette *fines herbes*. I also include it in every *bouquet garni*. And in the fresh, chopped herbs that it is nice to add at the last moment to gravy in a casserole that has cooked a bird.

Elderflower

This doesn't exactly fit into any category in *Gardener Cook* but who cares? I have never tasted any product of elderberries that I should like to repeat, but the flowers impart a delicious flavour of muscatel, commonly used in gooseberry jelly, but also in other ways.

The common elder, *Sambucus nigra*, flowers in June, but has quite a long six weeks' season. Not all the corymbs (flat-headed flower clusters) on one tree flower simultaneously, and not every tree at quite the same time as others placed, perhaps, in more or in less sun or shade. Basically, it is a widespread, bird-sown weed, and thus ubiquitous, especially in waste ground (rabbits leave it alone) and in hedgerows.

Gather the flower heads from a clean area, not where they'll be impregnated with the dust raised by traffic nor by exhaust fumes. Look critically at which corymbs you are picking. Still in bud is no use and you want to gather them before the petals start to fall. There is a right moment between these stages that probably lasts for a mere two days. Tap the corymbs free of insects.

There are several varieties of elder grown in gardens, equally for their foliage and for their flowers. The cut-leaved 'Laciniata' has large corymbs, and would be my first choice in the kitchen. After a number of years, a tree will become tired-looking, with smaller flower heads. You can cut it back in winter, quite ruthlessly, but will lose your crop for a year as a consequence.

Alternatively, and preferably, you can do some annual winter pruning by thinning, which will enable a continuous rejuvenation of your tree. Remove all those branches which flowered in the previous summer, leaving the young, unbranched shoots intact.

The other variety, which I use for elderflower cordial, is 'Guincho Purple'. Its pale flowers show up well against rich purple foliage. But there is, in fact, some colour in the flowers themselves; not much, but the stamens are pinkish. This will give an attractive flush to the finished cordial.

The Canadian elder, *Sambucus canadensis* 'Maxima', flowers later in the summer, at the tips of its young shoots. Its scent is similar to that of the common elder and I wonder if it might not prolong the cordial season, but I am currently without a bush, so have not tried.

ELDERFLOWER CORDIAL

I gave a recipe for this drink in *The Year at Great Dixter,* but nowadays use more lemon and less sugar, finding this more refreshing.

6 large elderflower heads, newly opened
5 large lemons
1¾ cups sugar
5 quarts boiling water

Put the elderflower heads into a large pan, with the lemons, cut in half and squeezed. (If the lemons are hard to squeeze, pour boiling water over them in a basin and leave for a couple of minutes, before cutting them open.) Add the sugar and pour in the water. Stir, cover and leave in a cool place for 3 days. Strain into bottles and it is ready to drink. Best to keep it chilled in the refrigerator, otherwise it lasts for only a few days, though seldom given the chance.

ELDERFLOWER SORBET

Colin Hamilton gave me this recipe. He is passionate about sorbets.

1¼ cups sugar
1¼ cups water
Handful of elderflower heads
Juice of 2 or 3 lemons
1 extra-large egg white

Set a pan containing the sugar and water over a low heat and stir gently until the sugar has dissolved. Stop stirring, increase the heat, and simmer for 5 minutes. Remove from the heat and drop in a handful of elderflowers. Leave to cool.

Strain the syrup and add the lemon juice. Pour the mixture into a shallow ice tray and freeze for about 3 hours, until firm. Remove from the freezer and chop up the syrup mixture. Beat the egg white until stiff, add the chopped-up mixture and beat hard until smooth. Return to the freezer.

The cut-leaved elder, Sambucus nigra *'Laciniata'*

248

Index

Index

Editor: Jo Christian
Designer: Sandra Wilson
Production: Peter Hinton
Indexer: Roger Owen
Head of Pictures: Anne Fraser

Editorial Director: Erica Hunningher
Art Director: Caroline Hillier
Production Director: Nicky Bowden